In school, you're a sup... every day – your powe. .5 knowledge!

If school gives you lemons, make lemonade and sell it at recess!

NAME:

AGE:

SCHOOL:

JOKES TO SHARE WITH YOUR FAMILY & FRIENDS

Why was the computer cold? **It left its Windows open!**

Why did the math book look so sad? **It had too many problems.**

What's the king of all school supplies? **The ruler!**

Why did the student eat his homework? **Because the teacher said it was a piece of cake!**

What's the best place to grow flowers in school? **In kinderGarden!**

What did the pencil say to the paper? **Write on!**

Date _____   Name _____

Get To Know Me!

Favorite Subject(s): [e.g., Math, Science, History, Grammar, Health, etc.]

_____

What would you like to learn more about this school year?

_____

_____

How do you prefer to learn new things?

[ ] Reading books and articles
[ ] Watching videos and documentaries
[ ] Doing hands-on experiments
[ ] Going on nature walks and exploring
[ ] Other (please specify):

_____

Are there any educational trips, such as exhibits, guided tours, or activities, that you are interested in attending during this academic year?

_____

_____

Anything else you'd like to share about your love for school or any subject?

_____

_____

_____

Score: _____

Date:_____

Simplifying Numerical
Expressions Involving Integers

mplifying numerical expressions with integers means making them easier to understand and solve. First, look
any operations inside parentheses and solve those. Next, do any multiplication or division from left to right,
d then handle addition or subtraction from left to right. This order helps you know which part to solve first. In the
d, you'll have a simpler expression or just one number!

oose the correct answer for each question below. Need more help? Try Google.

1. What is the result of 8 + (-3)?

    a. 11

    b. 3

    c. 5

2. What is the value of -7 + 2?

    a. -5

    b. -3

    c. -9

3. Simplify: 15 - 4 + (-6)

    a. 5

    b. 7

    c. 11

4. Calculate: -10 + 10 - 5

    a. 5

    b. 0

    c. -5

5. What is the result of 6 * (-2)?

    a. 12

    b. 8

    c. -12

6. What is -3 + (-7)?

    a. -12

    b. -5

    c. -10

7. Simplify: 4 - 9 + 2

    a. -3

    b. 1

    c. -5

8. What is the value of 12 / (-4)?

    a. -3

    b. 3

9. Calculate: -5 * 3 + 7

    a. 2

    b. -8

    c. -2

10. What is the result of 20 + (-8) + (-4)?

    a. 8

    b. 12

    c. 16

Identify the Adverb(s)

Instructions: Read each sentence carefully. Identify the adverb(s) in each sentence.

Adverbs are like the sprinkles on a cupcake! They add extra flavor to our sentences.

How: Adverbs can tell us how something happens. For example, in the sentence "She runs quickly," the word "quickly" is an adverb that tells us how she runs.

When: Adverbs can tell us when something happens. For example, in the sentence "I will do my homework later," the word "later" is an adverb that tells us when I will do my homework.

Where: Adverbs can tell us where something happens. For example, in the sentence "He is waiting outside," the word "outside" is an adverb that tells us where he is waiting.

To What Extent: Adverbs can tell us to what extent something happens. For example, in the sentence "She is very happy," the word "very" is an adverb that tells us to what extent she is happy.

1. She sings beautifully. _____

2. He runs quickly. _____

3. They always eat dinner together. _____

4. She rarely watches television. _____

5. The dog barks loudly. _____

6. He drives carefully. _____

7. She often reads books. _____

8. The cat quietly sneaked in. _____

9. He usually wakes up early. _____

10. She answered the question correctly. _____

11. He never forgets his keys. _____

12. The bird flew high. _____

13. She always brushes her teeth twice a day. _____

14. He slowly opened the door. _____

15. They happily played in the park. _____

Nucleic Acids

cleic acids are special molecules found in all living things that carry genetic information. They include DNA and RNA, which
build and run our bodies by storing and transmitting instructions for making proteins. Think of them as nature's blueprints
life!

d help? Try Google or your favorite search engine.

ross

. A unit of heredity that holds information to build and maintain an organism's cells.

. A protein that speeds up chemical reactions in the body, including those involving nucleic acids.

. A sugar molecule that forms part of RNA.

. A nitrogenous base found in RNA but not in DNA.

. Non-coding sections of DNA or RNA that are removed before translation into proteins.

Down

2. The shape of DNA, which looks like a twisted ladder.

3. A sequence of three DNA or RNA nucleotides that corresponds to a specific amino acid.

5. The complete set of DNA in an organism, containing all its genes.

6. The cell part where DNA is stored and protected.

9. Sections of DNA or RNA that code for proteins.

EXONS   URACIL   GENOME
HELIX   NUCLEUS   RIBOSE
INTRONS   GENE   ENZYME
CODON

The Haitian Revolution

The Haitian Revolution, which lasted from 1791 to 1804, was a successful slave revolt that took place in the French colony of Saint-Domingue, now known as Haiti. Enslaved Africans, led by figures like Toussaint Louverture, fought against the brutal conditions imposed by French colonial rule. Inspired by the ideals of the French Revolution, they sought freedom and equality. Despite fierce resistance from French forces, the revolutionaries eventually declared independence on January 1, 1804, making Haiti the first nation founded by formerly enslaved people. This revolution not only ended slavery in Haiti but also had a profound impact on abolitionist movements worldwide. It remains a powerful symbol of resistance and the fight for human rights.

	A	B	C	D
1.	Haittian	Hiatian	Haitian	Hiattian
2.	Revult	Revullt	Revolt	Revollt
3.	Fredum	Fredom	Freadom	Freedom
4.	Eqaullity	Equality	Equallity	Eqaulity
5.	Independense	Independanse	Independance	Independence
6.	Abolision	Abollision	Abollition	Abolition
7.	Collonial	Colonial	Colonail	Collonail
8.	Toossaint	Tousaint	Toussaint	Toosaint
9.	Looverture	Louverture	Louverrture	Looverrture
10.	Resistance	Resistence	Ressistence	Ressistance
11.	Enslaved	Ensclaved	Ensslaved	Enslavad
12.	Revolusion	Revollution	Revollusion	Revolution
13.	Siantt-Domingue	Saintt-Domingue	Siant-Domingue	Saint-Domingue
14.	Brrotal	Brotal	Brrutal	Brutal
15.	Victory	Victury	Victtury	Victtory

Science Spelling Words & Their Meanings

oose the correct answer for each question below. Need more help? Try Google.

1. What is the correct spelling of the term for the study of living organisms?
   a. Bioloyg
   b. Biolgy
   c. Biology

2. What is the correct spelling of the term that describes the force that attracts objects toward each other?
   a. Gravety
   b. Gravity
   c. Gravtiy

3. What is the correct spelling of the process by which plants make their food using sunlight?
   a. Photosinthesis
   b. Photosynthesis
   c. Photoesynthesis

4. What is the correct spelling of the term for the smallest unit of an element?
   a. Attom
   b. Atom
   c. Atem

5. What is the correct spelling of the scientific study of matter and its interactions?
   a. Chemestery
   b. Chemstry
   c. Chemistry

6. What is the correct spelling of the term for a substance made up of two or more different elements?
   a. Compound
   b. Compond
   c. Compund

7. What is the correct spelling of the process by which water vapor turns into liquid water?
   a. Condensaton
   b. Condensation
   c. Condenssation

8. What is the correct spelling of the scientific term for the study of the Earth's physical structure and substance?
   a. Geolgy
   b. Geoligy
   c. Geology

9. What is the correct spelling of the term for an organism that produces its own food?
   a. Autotroph
   b. Autotrophh
   c. Autotrof

10. What is the correct spelling of the term for the natural world, especially as affected by human activity?
    a. Enviroment
    b. Environment
    c. Enviorment

Art: Visual

First, read the entire passage. After that, go back and fill in the blanks. You can skip the blanks you're unsure about and finish them later.

splattering	Middle	ceramics	pencils	Greece
vases	inking	pharaohs'	oldest	three-dimensional

Visual arts are visible art forms such as drawing, painting, sculpture, printmaking, photography, and filmmaking. Desi
and textile work are also referred to as visual arts. The visual arts have evolved over time. During the
_____ Ages, artists became well-known for their paintings, sculptures, and prints. Today, visual arts
encompasses a wide range of disciplines.

Drawing is the process of creating a picture with a variety of tools, most commonly _____, crayons, pen
or markers. Artists draw on a variety of surfaces, such as paper or canvas. The first drawings were discovered in cave
around 30,000 years ago.

The ancient Egyptians drew on papyrus, while the Greeks and Romans drew on other objects such as
_____. Drawings were sketches made on parchment in the Middle Ages. Drawing became an art form
when paper became widely available during the Renaissance, and it was perfected by Michelangelo, Leonardo Da Vir
and others.

Painting is frequently referred to as the most important form of visual art. It's all about _____ paint on a
canvas or a wall. Painters use a variety of colors and brush strokes to convey their ideas.

Painting is one of the _____ forms of visual art as well. Prehistoric people painted hunting scenes on the
walls of old caves. Paintings became popular in ancient Egypt, where _____ tombs were adorned with
scenes from everyday Egyptian life.

Printmaking is a type of art that is created by _____ a plate and pressing it against the surface of anothe
object. Prints are now mostly made on paper, but they were originally pressed onto cloth or other objects. Plates are
frequently made of wood or metal.

Sculptures are _____ works of art created by shaping various materials. Stone, steel, plastic,
_____, and wood are among the most popular. Sculpture is frequently referred to as the plastic arts.
Sculpture can be traced back to ancient _____. Over many centuries, it has played an essential role in
various religions around the world. During the Renaissance, Michelangelo was regarded as one of the masters of the
art. David, a marble statue of a naked man, was his most famous work.

Music: Musical Terms

Score: _____

Date: _____

[complete the crossword by filling in a word that fits each clue. Fill in the correct answers, one letter per square, both across and down, from the [clues]. There will be a gray space between multi-word answers.

Solve the easy clues first, and then go back and answer the more difficult ones.

[Cr]oss

- [the] highest adult male singing voice; singing falsetto
- [the] part of a song that transitions between two main parts
- [a] combination of three or more tones sounded simultaneously
- [making up the song or melody as you play
- [,] a song written for one or more instruments playing solo
- [,] the highest of the singing voices
- [,] is a poem set to music with a recurring pattern of both rhyme and meter
- [,] timing or speed of the music

Down

1. singing without any instruments
3. low, the lowest of the voices and the lowest part of the harmony
6. to play a piece of music sweetly, tender, adoring manner
7. the sound of two or more notes heard simultaneously
9. is a musical interval; the distance between one note
10. played by a single musical instrument or voice
15. a range of voice that is between the bass and the alto
16. the repeating changing of the pitch of a note

CHORD   BRIDGE   ALTO
HARMONY   SOPRANO
IMPROVISATION   DOLCE
OCTAVE   VIBRATO   STANZA
SONATA   A CAPPELLA   TEMPO
BASS   SOLO   TENOR

Why It's Important To Apologize:
The Power Of Saying Sorry

Score: _____

Date: _____

In this activity, you'll see lots of grammatical *errors*. Correct all the grammar mistakes you see.

There are **9** mistakes in this passage. 0 capitals missing. 2 unnecessary capitals. 2 repeated words. 1 incorrect homophone. 4 incorrectly spelled words.

While it might be difficult to apologize, doing so is a crucial step in mending broken bonds and fostering new connections with others. A genuine apology shows concern for the person we have wronged while also accepti responsibility for our actions.

Sincere apologies demonstrate how much we care about the the other person by demonstrating that we are willing to take take responsibility for our actions and work toward repairing the damage we may hive caused. By doing So, we can begin to restore our mutual trust and create more respectful relationships wath won another.

On the other hand, if you dun't apologize when you shoold, you could end up doing more harm than good and damaging relationships To the point where trust is impossible to regain for years.

As a result, it's important to learn how and when to apologize so that you may improve your communication and strengthen your bonds with others in your personal and professional lives.

Order of Operations Pretest

en it comes to math you should always do your problems in the right order. If you don't work your problems in correct order you may end up with the wrong answer. Basically, the order of operations means the correct er in math.

1. Do everything _____ of brackets first.

   a. it doesn't matter which one you do first

   b. outside

   c. inside

2. When working with multiplication and division, you should perform them_____.

   a. right to left

   b. right or left

   c. left to right

3. For the problem 30 + 1 - 2 x 7 + 6 ÷ (5 x 2), what portion of the problem would you do first?

   a. Do the addition.

   b. Do the multiplication.

   c. Do the brackets.

4. For the problem 5 x 10 - (12 x 8 - 10) + 3 x 10 ÷ 5, how do you work the brackets?

   a. It don't matter which one I do first.

   b. Do the subtraction in the brackets first.

   c. Do the multiplication in the brackets first.

5. When working with addition and subtraction, you should perform them_____.

   a. neither left or right

   b. right to left

   c. left to right

6. If you have a bunch of operations of the same rank, you would operate from_____.

   a. left to right

   b. right to left

   c. both a and b

7. First, I do all operations that lie inside parentheses or brackets, then I_____.

   a. do any work with addition and subtraction

   b. do any work with exponents or radicals

   c. do any work from right to left

Comparative Adjectives

Comparative adjectives help us compare two things to show which has more or less of a certain quality. We usually add "-er" to the end of an adjective to make it comparative, like "taller" or "smaller." If the adjective is lor like "beautiful," we use "more" before it instead, like "more beautiful." We use the word "than" to show what we are comparing, like "Sarah is taller than John." This way, we can talk about the differences between things easi

Choose the correct answer for each question below. Need more help? Try Google.

1. What is the comparative form of 'big'?

    a. more big

    b. bigger

    c. biggest

2. Which of the following is the correct comparativ form of 'good'?

    a. gooder

    b. more good

    c. better

3. How do you form the comparative of 'happy'?

    a. more happy

    b. happier

    c. happyer

4. What is the comparative form of 'bad'?

    a. badder

    b. more bad

    c. worse

5. Which comparative form is correct for 'fast'?

    a. faster

    b. fastest

    c. more fast

6. What is the comparative of 'funny'?

    a. more funny

    b. funnier

    c. funniest

7. What is the correct comparative form of 'tall'?

    a. tallest

    b. more tall

    c. taller

8. Which of these is the comparative form of 'easy'?

    a. more easy

    b. easiest

    c. easier

9. What is the comparative form for 'old'?

    a. oldest

    b. more old

    c. older

10. What is the correct comparative form of 'rich'?

    a. more rich

    b. richer

    c. richest

Exoplanets

oplanets are planets that orbit stars outside our solar system. They come in various sizes and types, me similar to Earth and others vastly different. Scientists discover exoplanets using telescopes and ecial techniques like the transit method, where they observe a star's light dimming as a planet passes in nt of it. Studying exoplanets helps us understand more about how planets form and whether life might st elsewhere in the universe. Many exoplanets are found within a "habitable zone," where conditions uld support liquid water. Learning about exoplanets expands our knowledge of the vast and diverse smos.

ections: Carefully circle the correct spelling combinations of words.

	A	B	C	D
1.	Exopllanet	Exoplanet	Exupllanet	Exuplanet
2.	Orbyt	Orrbit	Orrbyt	Orbit
3.	Telescope	Telessope	Tellessope	Tellescope
4.	Trransit	Transit	Transyt	Trransyt
5.	Attmousphere	Atmousphere	Atmosphere	Attmosphere
6.	Habitible	Habittible	Habittable	Habitable
7.	Dettecsion	Dettection	Detection	Detecsion
8.	Lightt-yaer	Light-year	Light-yaer	Lightt-year
9.	Disssovery	Disscovery	Dissovery	Discovery
10.	Specttroscopy	Specttrouscopy	Spectroscopy	Spectrouscopy
11.	Asstronomy	Astronomy	Asctronomy	Astrunomy
12.	Pllanetary	Pllanetari	Planetari	Planetary
13.	Univerrse	Univerrce	Universe	Univerce
14.	Celestail	Cellestial	Cellestail	Celestial
15.	Extraterrestrail	Extraterestrail	Extraterrestrial	Extraterestrial

Henry Ford

During this exercise, fill in the blanks with the correct word. Need help? Try Google or your favorite search engine.

Innovation	Model	Innovation	machines	vehicle
Pioneer	car	Michigan	Industrialist	Entrepreneur
quantities	manufacturing	Engineer	Efficiency	resources

1. Automobile - A _____ with an engine used for transporting people, like a car.

2. Assembly Line - A _____ method where a product is put together in steps by different workers.

3. Ford Motor Company - The _____ company founded by Henry Ford in 1903.

4. _____ T - The first affordable car made by Henry Ford, introduced in 1908.

5. _____ - The act of creating new ideas or methods.

6. Detroit - The city in _____ where Henry Ford started his car company.

7. _____ - A person who designs and builds complex products, like cars.

8. Efficiency - Doing something in the best way with the least waste of time and _____.

9. Mass Production - Making large _____ of a product quickly and cheaply.

10. _____ - A person involved in the ownership and management of industries.

11. Mechanic - A person skilled in repairing and maintaining _____, especially cars.

12. _____ - Someone who is among the first to explore or settle a new area or develop new idea.

13. _____ - A person who starts and runs a business, taking on financial risks.

14. _____ - The introduction of new ideas, goods, services, and practices.

15. _____ - Achieving maximum productivity with minimum wasted effort or expense.

Today is Alphabetical Word Order Day!

phabetical order is a way to keep information in order. It makes it easier to find what you need. Additionally, anizing your spelling words alphabetically will assist you in remembering your word list.

arrange words alphabetically, starting with the first letter of each word. If a word begins with the same letter as other, you should evaluate the second letter. In some instances, if two or more words share the same first and cond letters, you may need to consider the third letter.

refully put the words in alphabetical order.

executive	1. _____
analysis	2. _____
reprimand	3. _____
hygiene	4. _____
ordinarily	5. _____
informant	6. _____
atmosphere	7. _____
mysterious	8. _____
receipt	9. _____
morale	10. _____
candidate	11. _____
humid	12. _____
management	13. _____
achievement	14. _____
politely	15. _____
kettle	16. _____
acres	17. _____

In this exercise, you'll need to write a sentence with each spelling word.

Art: Pablo Picasso

French	angles	depressed	life	collaborated
painting	Spanish	sand	Barcelona	influence
painter	Carlos	blue	circuses	suicide
newspapers	dream	Madrid	historians	prestigious
recovered	died	classical-style	greatest	features

blo Picasso was born on October 25, 1881, in Spain and grew up there. His father was a _____ who also taught art. Pablo has always enjoyed drawing since he was a child. cording to legend, his first word was "piz," which is _____ for "pencil." Pablo quickly monstrated that he had little interest in school but was an extremely talented artist. Pablo enrolled in _____ art school in _____ when he was fourteen years old. He nsferred to another school in _____ a few years later. Pablo, on the other hand, was satisfied with the traditional art school teachings. He didn't want to paint in the manner of people m hundreds of years ago. He wished to invent something new.

blo's close friend _____ Casagemas committed _____ in 1901. Pablo became _____. He began painting in Paris around the same time. For the next four years, the or _____ dominated his paintings. Many of the subjects appeared depressed and solemn. He picted people with elongated _____ and faces in his paintings. Poor People on the ashore and The Old Guitarist are two of his paintings from this time.

blo eventually _____ from his depression. He also had feelings for a _____ model. He began to use warmer colors such as pinks, reds, oranges, and beiges in his intings. The Rose Period is a term used by art _____ to describe this period in blo's life. He also started painting happier scenes like _____. The Peasants and ther and Child are two of his paintings from this time period.

casso began experimenting with a new _____ style in 1907. He _____ with another artist, Georges Braque. By 1909, they had developed a mpletely new painting style known as Cubism. Cubism analyzes and divides subjects into different ctions. The sections are then reassembled and painted from various perspectives and _____.

casso began combining Cubism and collage in 1912. He would use _____ or plaster in his paint give it texture in this area. He would also add dimension to his paintings by using materials such as lored paper, _____, and wallpaper. Three Musicians and the Portrait of Ambroise

Vollard are two of Picasso's Cubism paintings.

Although Picasso continued to experiment with Cubism, he went through a period of painting more _____ paintings around 1921. He was influenced by Renaissance painters such as Raphael. He created strong characters that appeared three-dimensional, almost like statues. The Pipes of Pan and Woman in White are two of his works in this style.

Pablo became interested in the Surrealist movement around 1924. Surrealist paintings were never meant to make sense. They frequently resemble something out of a nightmare or a _____. Although Picasso did not join the movement, he did incorporate some of its ideas into his paintings. This period was dubbed "Monster Period" by some. Guernica and The Red Armchair are two examples of surrealism's _____ on Picasso's art.

Pablo Picasso is widely regarded as the greatest artist of the twentieth century. Many consider him to be one of the _____ artists in all of history. He painted in a variety of styles and made numerous unique contributions to the world of art. He painted several self-portraits near the end of his _____. Self-Portrait Facing Death, a self-portrait done with crayons on paper, was one of his final works of art. He _____ a year later, on April 8, 1973, at the age of 91.

Music: String Family Instruments

Score: _____

Date: _____

ngs vibrate to produce sound in stringed instruments. Stringed instruments come in a wide variety of styles, from guitars to
ns to zithers to harps. Stringed instruments vibrate their strings to produce sound. Strings vibrate in different ways
ending on the type of instrument being played.

cking the strings is one way to make them vibrate. When a guitarist uses their fingers, hands, or a pick to cause the string to
ate and produce sound, this is how the guitar sounds. The harp, banjo, lute, and sitar are among the other instruments that
be performed in this manner. Picking and strumming are other terms for plucking.

ny stringed instruments are played by stroking a bow over the strings. It's not uncommon for bows to be made from long
ks with a substance woven into them, most commonly horsehair. The movement of the material down the string produces a
nd and vibration. Violin, cello, and fiddle are examples of instruments that use a bow as their primary sound source.

smallest string instrument is the violin and the biggest string instrument is the double bass.

V	H	J	C	B	G	Y	I	G	R	Q	T
M	W	V	Q	A	D	T	C	E	L	L	O
A	K	P	P	N	O	T	S	J	K	W	V
N	Z	V	V	J	U	U	U	J	F	Q	D
D	S	Q	I	O	B	V	H	A	R	P	S
O	F	X	O	U	L	Q	U	B	H	B	O
L	K	Z	L	K	E	H	G	M	J	F	E
I	R	C	A	U	B	V	I	O	L	I	N
N	S	B	P	L	A	Y	J	V	E	B	U
Y	B	O	G	E	S	U	O	I	N	O	O
P	J	B	K	L	S	I	Z	C	M	N	X
A	Q	W	T	E	S	U	A	A	E	N	E

Violin   Viola   Cello   Double Bass

Harp   Banjo   Mandolin   Ukulele

Paranoia

In this activity, you'll see lots of grammatical *errors*. Correct all the grammar mistakes you see.

There are **9** mistakes in this passage. 1 capital missing. 2 unnecessary capitals. 1 repeated word. 1 incorrect homophone. 4 incorrectly spelled words.

Paranoia behavior is a psychological condition where someone feels haghly suspicious and fearful of thé world around tham. It differs from from healthy caution and can impede normal functioning, making it difficult for those with paranoia to participate in meaningful relationships or just get through a typical day. the most important thing to remember about paraniod behavior is that it can also be a symptom of larger mental health issues and should be discussed with a professional to ensure proper support is in place.

Thoughts of suspicion are not always the result of paranoia. There are times when we should all be wary and suspicious. It's perfectly Reasonable too suspect something, provided you have good reason to do so. If, for instance, a large number of people on your street have been victimized, it is reasonable to be cautious about Your persunal safety when strolling around. An accurate suspicion of danger can save your life.

One-Tenth or One-Hundredth
More or Less

Score: _____

Date:_____

e-tenth means dividing something into 10 equal parts, and one-hundredth means dividing it into 100 equal parts. If you have -tenth more, you're adding a small piece (1 out of 10) to your total. If it's one-tenth less, you're taking away that same small ce. One-hundredth more or less works the same way, but the pieces are even smaller, since 100 parts are smaller than 10 s. So, you're adjusting the amount by tiny bits!

pose the correct answer for each question below. Need help? Try Google.

1. What is one-tenth of 100?

    a. 5

    b. 20

    c. 10

2. If you have 50 and you take away one-tenth, how much do you have left?

    a. 55

    b. 45

    c. 40

3. What is one-hundredth of 2500?

    a. 2.5

    b. 25

    c. 250

4. If a product costs $200 and is marked down by one-hundredth, what is the new price?

    a. $198

    b. $199

    c. $200

5. What is one-tenth more than 30?

    a. 28

    b. 31

    c. 33

6. If you have 80 and you add one-tenth of it, what is the total?

    a. 76

    b. 90

    c. 88

7. What is one-hundredth less than 1?

    a. 0.90

    b. 1.01

    c. 0.99

8. How much is one-tenth of 450?

    a. 40

    b. 50

    c. 45

9. If a value is decreased by one-hundredth, what is the new value of 500?

    a. 499.99

    b. 505

    c. 500.01

10. What is one-tenth of 900?

    a. 90

    b. 100

    c. 80

Learning Comma Usage

Score: _____

Date: _____

Commas with a Series: Use commas to separate items in a series or list.

 Example: I bought apples, bananas, and oranges at the store.

Commas with Dates: Use a comma to separate the day of the week and the day, and another comma to separate the day from the year.

 Example: We will have a picnic on Saturday, April 15, 2023.

Commas with the Names of Places: Use commas to separate the name of a city from the state, and to separate the city or state from the country.

 Example: He lives in Portland, Oregon, United States.

Commas with Direct Addresses: Use commas to set off the name of a person being directly addressed in a sentence.

 Example: John, could you please pass the salt?

Write "correct" if the sentence is correct as is. If incorrect, rewrite the sentence correctly.

1. I want to buy pencils, erasers and notebooks. _____

2. We went to the beach on Monday June 5 2023. _____

3. My friend Mary lives in New York New York. _____

4. Mom, can you please help me with my homework? _____

5. We visited Paris, France, last summer. _____

6. We need to buy milk eggs and bread from the store. _____

7. The party is on Saturday, April 20, 2024. _____

8. Sarah, could you pass me the scissors? _____

9. The dog named Spot lives in Los Angeles California United States. _____

10. We enjoyed pizza hamburgers and fries at the party. _____

11. I was born on Tuesday May 10 2010. _____

12. Please hand me the book Anna. _____

13. Our school is located in London England United Kingdom. _____

14. The cat named Whiskers is hiding under the bed. _____

15. Last year, we went on a vacation to Tokyo, Japan. _____

Rock Cycle

t, read all the way through. After that, go back and fill in the blanks. You can skip the blanks you're unsure about and finish them
r.

tectonic	transformed	lava	particles	chemically
erosion	metamorphic	time	layers	shale

e rock cycle is a continuous process that describes how rocks are formed, broken down, and
_____ over time. This cycle helps explain the dynamic nature of Earth's crust and the
erent types of rocks we find.

ere are three main types of rocks: igneous, sedimentary, and _____. Each type forms
ough different processes and can be transformed into another type over _____.

eous rocks form from the cooling and solidification of molten rock, called magma or
_____. When magma cools slowly beneath the Earth's surface, it forms intrusive
eous rocks like granite. If lava cools quickly on the surface, it creates extrusive igneous rocks like
salt.

dimentary rocks are formed from the accumulation of small _____, like sand, silt, and
y, which are carried by wind, water, or ice and deposited in _____. Over time, these
ers become compacted and cemented together, forming rocks like sandstone, shale, and
estone. Sedimentary rocks often contain fossils, which provide clues about Earth's past life and
vironments.

tamorphic rocks are created when existing rocks are subjected to heat and pressure, causing them
change physically and _____ without melting. This transformation can occur deep
hin the Earth or at _____ plate boundaries. Examples of metamorphic rocks include
rble, which forms from limestone, and schist, which forms from _____.

e rock cycle is driven by Earth's internal heat, gravitational forces, and external processes like
athering and _____. For example, igneous rocks can be broken down into sediments
weathering and erosion, eventually forming sedimentary rocks. These sedimentary rocks can be
ried and subjected to heat and pressure, transforming into metamorphic rocks. If the conditions are
ht, metamorphic rocks can melt and become magma, starting the cycle anew.

The Mayflower Compact

The Mayflower Compact was a written agreement created by the Pilgrims in 1620. It was signed aboard the Mayflower, their ship, before they landed at Plymouth in present-day Massachusetts. The document established basic form of government and laws for the new colony. It emphasized the importance of working together for the common good. The Mayflower Compact is significant because it was one of the first steps toward self-government in America. It set a precedent for future democratic practices in the colonies.

	A	B	C	D
1.	Mayfflower	Meyfflower	Mayflower	Meyflower
2.	Cumpactt	Compactt	Compact	Cumpact
3.	Pillgrims	Pilgrims	Pylgrims	Pyllgrims
4.	Plymooth	Pllymooth	Pllymouth	Plymouth
5.	Agreement	Agrenment	Agreient	Agreement
6.	Culony	Cullony	Colony	Collony
7.	Shipbuard	Shipboard	Shipboarrd	Shipbuarrd
8.	Goverrnment	Government	Goverrment	Goverment
9.	Lawsc	Lews	Laws	Lawss
10.	Precedent	Presedent	Prrecedent	Prresedent
11.	Demucracy	Democrracy	Demucrracy	Democracy
12.	Settlement	Setlement	Sottlonmont	Sctlcnmcnt
13.	Signerrs	Signers	Sygners	Sygnerrs
14.	Leaderrship	Leadership	Laedership	Laederrship
15.	Ameryca	Amerryca	America	Amerrica

Today Is Spelling Day! Spelling Words Sort

Name: _____

Date: _____

habetical order is a way to keep information in order. It makes it easier to find what you need. Additionally, anizing your spelling words alphabetically will assist you in remembering your word list.

arrange words alphabetically, starting with the first letter of each word. If a word begins with the same letter as other, you should evaluate the second letter. In some instances, if two or more words share the same first and cond letters, you may need to consider the third letter.

refully put these words in alphabetical order.

cinnamon	1. _____
idol	2. _____
elementary	3. _____
category	4. _____
concentrate	5. _____
inherit	6. _____
committed	7. _____
capital	8. _____
fabricate	9. _____
heroic	10. _____
boundary	11. _____
innocent	12. _____
irate	13. _____
baggage	14. _____
athlete	15. _____

Art: Roman Portrait Sculptures

Alexander	aristocrats	ancestral	shrine	rewarded
sculpture	pattern	mosaics	marble	artistic

Portrait _____ has been practiced since the beginning of Roman history. It was mos
likely influenced by the Roman practice of creating _____ images. When a Roman
man died, his family made a wax sculpture of his face and kept it in a special _____ at hom
Because these sculptures were more like records of a person's life than works of art, the emphasis
was on realistic detail rather than _____ beauty.

As Rome became more prosperous and gained access to Greek sculptors, Roman
_____ known as patricians began creating these portraits from stone rather tha
wax.

Roman sculpture was about more than just honoring the dead; it was also about honoring the living.
Important Romans were _____ for their valor or greatness by having statues of
themselves erected and displayed in public. This is one of the earliest of these types of statues that
we've discovered, and the _____ continued all the way until the Republic's demise.

The mosaic is the only form of Roman art that has yet to be discussed. The Romans adored mosaic
and created them with exquisite skill. The Romans created _____ of unprecedented qua
and detail using cubes of naturally colored _____. The floor mosaic depicting
_____ the Great at the Battle of Issus is probably the most famous Roman mosaic.

Sound Waves Crossword

nd waves are a form of mechanical wave, meaning they require a medium to travel through. The speed of sound is affected he properties of the medium it is traveling through, such as temperature, pressure, and density.

ch the clues to the words. Need help? Try Google.

ross

A rapid movement or shaking of the air that produces sound or a sensation of movement.

The thin membranes in the inner ear that vibrate in response to sound waves and help the brain interpret them as sounds.

A period of 100 years.

The way a person behaves or acts in response to a particular situation or event.

To transmit information, such as audio or video, over radio waves so it can be received by multiple people simultaneously.

Down

3. Someone who is devoted to studying, researching, and understanding the fundamental nature of knowledge, reality, and existence.

5. The act of discovering something that was previously unknown.

6. People engaged in research and experimentation with the aim of gaining new knowledge about different topics.

8. Small electronic devices designed to make life easier or more enjoyable.

9. Pleasingly attractive, especially in appearance; having qualities that delight the senses and stir emotion

PHILOSOPHER   BEAUTIFUL
BROADCAST   EARDRUMS
GADGETS   VIBRATION
CENTURY   DISCOVERY
SCIENTISTS   BEHAVIOR

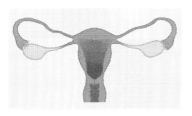

Reproductive Health Words You Should Know

Match the clues to the words. Need help? Try Google.

Across

3. The process of childbirth.
5. The first time a person gets their period.
7. A breast/chest cancer screening that takes x-rays of the breasts/chest tissue to find lumps.
8. The tightening and releasing of the muscles that stop urination in order to prevent and improve urinary incontinence.
9. The inability to become pregnant or to cause a pregnancy.

Down

2. A treatment that prevents cervical cancer.
4. The lips of the vulva.
5. A health care provider who is trained to assist in childbirth.
6. Menstrual bleeding that's heavier or longer lasting than usual.
9. Being unable to control urination or bowel movements.

LABOR   LABIA   INFERTILITY
MAMMOGRAM
MENORRHAGIA   MIDWIFE
INCONTINENCE   LEEP
MENARCHE   KEGEL
EXERCISES

Conversions

Sentence Building: Unscramble the sentences!

(Use a separate sheet of paper to write out sentences if needed.)

1. _____

centimeters.   another,   to   changing   inches   measurement   Conversions   involve   to   one   of   unit   like

2. _____

to   To   you   kilometers,   multiply   by   convert   from   miles   the   miles   1.60934   of   number

3. _____

and   conversions   everyday   in   Understanding   life.   important   math,   science,   is

4. _____

to   In   tablespoons   need   cooking,   convert   you   teaspoons.   might   to

5. _____

to   Fahrenheit   tricky;   a   can   converting   for   Celsius   Temperature   conversions   requires   example,   formula.   be

6. _____

pounds   When   to   the   2.20462   by   converting   you   from   of   pounds   divide   kilograms,   number

7. _____

easier   because   liters,   they   are   often   to   Metric   units,   use   system.   a   like   meters   base-10   and   convert

8. _____

to   when   Currency   of   conversions   different   countries.   people   money   the   traveling   value   help   understand

9. _____

conversion   Converting   of   type   mathematics.   decimals   common   a   fractions   to   in   is

10. _____

and   their   are   regularly   ensure   perform   measurements   accurate.   conversions   Engineers   to   architects

Types of Context Clues

Context clues are hints or information provided within a text that help readers understand the meaning of new or difficult words. These clues can be found in the words, sentences, or paragraphs surrounding the unfamiliar term. Being able to use context clues effectively is an important reading skill, as it allows readers to comprehend texts more fully, especially when they encounter new vocabulary.

Types of Context Clues and Examples

1. **Definition or Explanation Clues:** The unknown word is directly defined or explained within the sentence or in the following sentence.

   - **Example:** "The arboretum, a place where various trees and shrubs are grown for study, was open for a public tour."

   In this sentence, 'arboretum' is directly explained as "a place where various trees and shrubs are grown for study."

2. **Synonym or Restatement Clues:** A synonym or another form of restatement is used to define the unfamiliar word.

   - **Example:** "She felt lethargic, too sluggish and tired to complete her work."

   Here, 'sluggish and tired' are synonyms that help to understand 'lethargic.'

3. **Antonym or Contrast Clues:** The meaning is conveyed by contrasting the unfamiliar word with its opposite.

   - **Example:** "Unlike his gregarious sister, who loves socializing, Mark is quite introverted and prefers solitude."

   'Introverted' is contrasted with 'gregarious,' indicating it means something like being reserved or shy.

4. **Example Clues:** Specific examples are used to define the term.

   - **Example:** "Celestial bodies, such as the sun, moon, and stars, are always fascinating to astronomers."

   'Celestial bodies' are explained by giving examples like the sun, moon, and stars.

5. **Inference Clues:** Readers need to infer the meaning from the general context of the sentence or paragraph.

   - **Example:** "The children approached the haunted house hesitantly, their faces showing trepidation."

   The context implies that 'trepidation' means a feeling of fear or anxiety.

6. **Cause and Effect Clues:** The reason or outcome of a situation helps in defining the term.

   - **Example:** "Due to the drought, the ground was parched, so it cracked and crumbled easily."

   'Parched' implies that the ground is very dry, as it's a result of the drought.

Context Clues Multiple Choice Questions

Her obstinate nature meant she rarely changed her mind; once she made a decision, it was final." The word 'obstinate' most likely means:

. Flexible

. Stubborn

. Friendly

. Scared

He was an amateur astronomer; stargazing was more of a hobby than a profession for him." The word 'amateur' means someone who is:

. Professional

. Uninterested

. Experienced

. Non-professional

The cat, known for its stealth, moved silently as it approached its prey." The word 'stealth' means:

. Clumsiness

. Loudness

. Caution

. Secrecy

During the marathon, she felt so fatigued that she could barely finish the race." The word 'fatigued' means:

. Energized

. Exhausted

. Excited

. Focused

True or False Questions

He was known for his benevolence, always ready to help those in need." The word 'benevolence' means kindness.

True or False

6. "The aroma of freshly baked bread wafted from the kitchen." The word 'aroma' refers to an unpleasant smel

   True or False

7. "She was notorious for her punctuality, always arriving late to meetings." The word 'punctuality' means being time.

   True or False

8. "The antique vase was quite fragile, so it needed to be handled with great care." The word 'fragile' means durable.

   True or False

Short Answer Questions

9. What does 'innovative' mean in the sentence, "Steve Jobs was known for his innovative ideas, which often introduced new methods and inventions"?

---

10. Based on the sentence, "The guide spoke in a monotonous voice, making the tour rather dull," what does 'monotonous' mean?

---

11. In the sentence, "The chef's culinary skills were exceptional, as evidenced by the exquisite meal," what do 'culinary' relate to?

---

12. Define 'copious' as used in the sentence, "He took copious notes during the lecture to ensure he didn't miss any important information."

Soil Composition

Score: _____

Date: _____

I composition refers to what makes up soil, which is essential for plant growth. Soil is a mixture of
nerals, organic matter, water, and air. The minerals come from broken-down rocks, while organic matter
ludes decomposed plants and animals. Water and air in the soil help roots get the nutrients they need.
'erent types of soil, like sandy, clay, or loamy, have different compositions. Understanding soil
mposition helps us grow healthy plants and manage farmland effectively.

ections: Carefully circle the correct spelling combinations of words.

	A	B	C	D
1.	Mynerrals	Minerals	Minerrals	Mynerals
2.	Organyc	Orrganyc	Orrganic	Organic
3.	Homus	Humus	Humuss	Humusc
4.	Sandstune	Sandstone	Sandsctone	Sandsstone
5.	Luamy	Loamy	Lotmy	Laumy
6.	Textture	Textore	Texture	Texttore
7.	Porrosity	Porosity	Porrousity	Porousity
8.	Microbes	Micrubes	Micrrubes	Micrrobes
9.	Aerrasion	Aerration	Aerasion	Aeration
10.	Nutrients	Nuttreints	Nutreints	Nuttrients
11.	Erotion	Erosion	Errotion	Errosion
12.	Decompose	Decomposse	Decompouse	Decompousse
13.	Ferrtiliti	Ferrtility	Fertility	Fertiliti
14.	Sediment	Sedinment	Sedinmentt	Sedimentt
15.	Compactsion	Compacttion	Compacsion	Compaction

Cowboys and Outlaws

During this exercise, fill in the blanks with the correct word. Need help? Try Google or your favorite search engine.

criminal's	outlaw	Sheriff	Posse	animals
rope	Revolver	farm	Frontier	cows
wagon	law	Saloon	Duel	Cowboy

1. _____: A person who herds and tends cattle on a ranch, often on horseback.

2. Cattle: Large farm animals, like _____, that are raised for their meat or milk.

3. Ranch: A large _____ where cattle and other animals are raised.

4. Lasso: A long _____ with a loop used by cowboys to catch animals.

5. Outlaw: A person who breaks the _____ and lives outside of legal authority.

6. _____: An officer who keeps law and order in a town or county.

7. _____: A place where people in the Old West went to drink, eat, and socialize.

8. Bandit: Another word for an _____ who robs people.

9. _____: A group of people, usually led by a sheriff, who chase and capture criminals.

10. Wanted Poster: A sign showing a _____ picture and offering a reward for their capture.

11. _____: A fight between two people, often using guns, to settle a dispute.

12. _____: A type of handgun commonly used by cowboys and outlaws.

13. Herd: A group of _____, like cattle, that live and move together.

14. _____: The edge of settled land where pioneers lived and new areas were explored.

15. Stagecoach: A horse-drawn _____ used for carrying passengers and mail across the country.

Vocabulary: Community Services

Directions: Read the words. Sort the words into the community services in which they belong.

insurance	sick	injured	emergency	firefighter	doctor
driver's license	video	adult education	nurse	ticket	EMS worker
Principal	students	teacher	magazines	officer	return
loan	learning	junior high	borrow	newspapers	librarian
medicine	books	pharmacist	911	high school	pharmacy
elementary school					

Hospital (8)	Library (8)	Police/Fire Department (7)	School (8)

Art: Leonardo da Vinci

During the Italian Renaissance, Leonardo da Vinci was an artist, scientist, and inventor. Many people see him as one the most gifted and bright people of all time. Because of Leonardo's various talents, the term Renaissance Man (someone who excels in many areas) was coined, and it is now used to describe persons who resemble da Vinci.

Leonardo da Vinci is widely recognized as one of history's finest artists. Drawing, painting, and sculpture were among Leonardo's many talents. Despite the fact that we don't have many of his paintings today, he is arguably most known his paintings, which helped him earn prominence during his lifetime. The Mona Lisa and The Last Supper are two of h most famous works, and possibly two of the most famous in the world. For nearly 200 years, the 'Mona Lisa' has beer displayed in the Louvre gallery in Paris.

Leonardo spent his final three years in France and died in 1519 at **age 67** in the Loire Valley.

1. Where was he born?

   a. America

   b. England

   c. Italy

2. What was his first name?

   a. Leonardo

   b. Emilio

   c. Devinni

3. As a child, he wanted to_____?

   a. swim in the lake

   b. fly in the sky

   c. climb a mountain

4. He drew pictures of

   a. buildings

   b. food

   c. nature

5. How did he get better at drawing?

   a. He watched YouTube.

   b. He had a friend who helped.

   c. He studied.

6. His most famous painting is_____?

   a. Mona Dona

   b. Lisa Maria

   c. Mona Lisa

7. Leonardo was _____ handed.

   a. left

   b. used both hands

   c. right

8. The Mona Lisa is a portrait of the wife of a _____ official.

   a. United States

   b. Florentine

   c. Army

9. Who Stole the Mona Lisa?

   a. Vincenzo Peruggia

   b. Veronica Perkily

   c. Vincent Paisley

10. Can you buy the real Mona Lisa?

   a. The painting cannot be bought or sold according to French heritage law

   b. The painting is currently on sale for 1 million dollars.

   c. The painting can be brought at your loca art gallery.

MUSIC: The Orchestra Vocab Words

scramble the names of the instruments found in the orchestra.

violin	strings	double bass	harp	cello	clarinet
timpani	oboe	trumpet	piano	french horn	flute
bassoon	saxaphone	cymbals	xylophone	trombone	drums
woodwind	percussion	brass	conductor		

ueft   _ l _ _ _

invol   v _ o _ _ _

obeo   _ _ o _

nfrech honr   _ r _ _ _ _   h _ _ _

nabooss   _ _ _ _ o o _

rlniatce   _ _ a r _ _ _ _

sdrum   _ r _ _ _

nipmiat   _ i _ _ a _ _

nsrtgis   _ t _ _ n _ _

odonidww   _ o _ d _ _ _ _

asrbs   b _ _ _ _

12. rucspiosne   _ _ _ c u s _ _ _ _

13. eclol   _ _ l _ _

14. aprh   h _ _ _

15. edolub bssa   d _ _ _ _ e   _ _ _ s

16. eupmttr   _ _ _ m _ _ t

17. etbmoron   _ _ o _ _ _ _ e

18. phexloyno   x _ l _ _ _ _ _ _

19. lscmbay   _ _ _ _ a _ s

20. odornuctc   c _ _ _ _ c _ _ _

21. noapi   _ i _ _ _

22. phxasoaen   s _ x _ _ _ _ _ _

Heart Crossword

Match the clues to the words. Need help? Try Google.

Across

2. the act of hindering
4. part of an organism consisting of an aggregate of cells
6. the part of the human torso between the neck and the diaphragm
8. an object used as a container, especially for liquids
9. a physical feeling of suffering or discomfort

Down

1. identifying the nature or cause of some phenomenon
3. not typical or usual or regular
5. an act that does not succeed
7. the hollow muscular organ located behind the sternum

PREVENTION HEART
CHEST FAILURE
VESSEL PAIN
ABNORMAL DIAGNOSIS
TISSUE

Time Zones

e zones are like different parts of the world having their own clocks. Because the Earth is so big, the sun rises and sets at
erent times in different places. So, people in one place might be eating breakfast while others are already having dinner!
e zones help everyone know what time it is in different places. If you travel far, like from New York to London, you might
e to change your clock to match the new time zone.

Jose the correct answer for each question below. Need help? Try Google.

1. What is the time zone for New York City?

    a. Pacific Standard Time (PST)

    b. Eastern Standard Time (EST)

    c. Central Standard Time (CST)

2. Which time zone is 10 hours ahead of UTC?

    a. UTC+5

    b. UTC+10

    c. UTC-5

3. What time zone does London operate on during
Daylight Saving Time?

    a. Central European Time (CET)

    b. British Summer Time (BST)

    c. Greenwich Mean Time (GMT)

4. Which city is in the Central Time Zone?

    a. Chicago

    b. Los Angeles

    c. New York

5. When does Daylight Saving Time typically end in the
United States?

    a. Last Sunday in March

    b. First Sunday in November

    c. Last Sunday in October

6. What is the time difference between UTC and Indian
Standard Time?

    a. UTC+5

    b. UTC+5:30

    c. UTC+6

7. Which of the following regions does NOT observe
Daylight Saving Time?

    a. Hawaii

    b. California

    c. Florida

8. What is the time zone abbreviation for Japan?

    a. CST (China Standard Time)

    b. JST (Japan Standard Time)

    c. JDT (Japan Daylight Time)

9. Which time zone is used in the majority of western
Canada?

    a. Pacific Standard Time (PST)

    b. Mountain Standard Time (MST)

    c. Central Standard Time (CST)

10. What time zone is used in Brazil's capital, Brasília?

    a. Brasília Time (BRT)

    b. Amazon Time (AMT)

    c. Acre Time (ACT)

Identify The Various Parts of Grammar

Across

1. the first word in a noun group
2. a word used to describe a noun
3. the first part of a sentence is called the ....
7. this tells us how many of a noun (some / ten / a few)
10. a sentence that uses a conjunction to join two independent clauses
11. a sentence with a dependent clause and one or more independent clauses
12. one conjunction is ....
15. a clause beginning with if / when / because is called ....
18. the last part of a sentence is called ....
19. a phrase beginning with a preposition is called ....

Down

3. What type of sentence is one independent clause
4. an independent clause can only have one ....
5. The last word of a noun group
6. a / an / the are called
8. this / that / these / those are called ....
9. tells us who owns the noun
13. we change the verb to make past ....
14. a story written or spoken in past tense
16. a clause that contains the full meaning is called ....
20. the conjunctions so and because give us a result and ....

ADJECTIVE   INDEPENDENT
COMPLEX   TENSE   DEPENDENT
BECAUSE   VERB
POSSESSIVE   QUANTIFIER
COMPOUND   SIMPLE
PREPOSITIONAL   RECOUNT
DETERMINER   ARTICLE
OBJECT   REASON   SUBJECT
DEMONSTRATIVE   NOUN

Constellations

, read all the way through. After that, go back and fill in the blanks. You can skip the blanks you're unsure about and finish them

Major	seasons	navigation	Polaris	sky
Stargazing	orbits	astronomers	north	stars

nstellations are patterns of _____ in the night sky that people have imagined to look
e pictures or shapes. These star patterns have been used for thousands of years to tell stories,
vigate, and keep track of time.

ere are 88 official constellations recognized by _____ today. Each constellation has
own unique shape and story. For example, one of the most famous constellations is the Big Dipper,
ich looks like a large spoon or dipper. The Big Dipper is part of a larger constellation called Ursa
_____, or the Great Bear.

other well-known constellation is Orion, the Hunter. Orion is easy to spot because of the three
ght stars that form his "belt." You can also see his "shoulders" and "legs" made up of other bright
rs. According to Greek mythology, Orion was a great hunter who was placed in the
_____ by the gods.

nstellations are important for _____. Before modern technology, sailors and travelers
ed the stars to find their way. One very helpful constellation for navigation is the Little Dipper, which
ludes the North Star, or _____. Polaris always points _____ and helps
ople figure out which direction they are facing.

nstellations also help us keep track of time and _____. As Earth _____
e Sun, different constellations become visible at different times of the year. For instance, in the
iter, you might see Orion in the sky, while in the summer, you might see Scorpius, the Scorpion.

_____ is a fun activity that can help you learn more about constellations. All you need is
lear night sky and a little bit of patience. You can even use a star map or a stargazing app to help
u find and identify different constellations.

next time you look up at the night sky, try to spot some constellations and imagine the stories
hind them. It's like having a giant, sparkling picture book right above your head!

The Red Scare

During this exercise, fill in the blanks with the correct word. Need help? Try Google or your favorite search engine.

communism	atomic	Patriotism	Espionage	Loyalty
Fearmongering	Propaganda	Atomic	Subversion	Soviet
Iron	Cold	political	McCarthyism	Act

1. Red Scare - A period of intense fear of _____ in the United States.

2. Communism - A _____ system where all property is publicly owned, and each person works and is paid according to their abilities and needs.

3. _____ War - The rivalry between the United States and the Soviet Union after World War I which heightened fears of communism.

4. _____ - The practice of making accusations of subversion or treason without proper evidence, named after Senator Joseph McCarthy.

5. _____ Spies - Individuals accused of spying for the Soviet Union and passing information about the atomic bomb.

6. Smith _____ - A law that made it illegal to advocate for the violent overthrow of the government, used to target communists.

7. _____ Union - The communist nation that was a major adversary of the United States during the Cold War.

8. _____ - The act of spying, especially by government agents.

9. _____ - The act of trying to undermine the authority or integrity of an established system or institution.

10. _____ - Devotion to one's country; during the Red Scare, questioning someone's patriotism was common if they were suspected of communist sympathies.

11. Cold War _____ - Information, especially biased or misleading, used to promote anti-communist sentiments.

12. _____ Oaths - Pledges of allegiance to the United States, required of many government employees to prove they were not communists.

13. Rosenberg Trial - The trial of Julius and Ethel Rosenberg, who were executed for allegedly passing _____ secrets to the Soviet Union.

14. _____ Curtain - The metaphorical division between the communist nations of Eastern Euro and the democratic nations of Western Europe.

15. _____ - Spreading fear to influence public opinion, often used during the Red Scare to control attitudes toward communism.

Vocab Crossword Puzzle

Name: _____

Date: _____

[Logo graphic: SAUCE / APP / CAPITAL / FIELD / DE spelling "ACADEMIC"]

...ve the puzzle below with the correct vocabulary word.

[Crossword grid with numbered squares: 7, 4, 8, 2, 6, 9, 3, 10, 1, 5]

...ross

capability; ability; innate or acquired capacity for something;

to seize by or as if by authority; appropriate summarily:

to waste time; idle; trifle; loiter: to move slowly

the remains of anything broken down or destroyed; ruins; rubble:

heroic; majestic; impressively great:

■. something that is not what it purports to be; a spurious imitation; fraud or hoax.

Down

2. violently or destructively frenzied; wild; crazed; deranged:

7. to move or act with haste; proceed with haste; hurry:

8. portending evil or harm; foreboding; threatening; inauspicious:

9. having its original purity; uncorrupted or unsullied.

OMINOUS   DEBRIS
APTITUDE   BERSERK
SHAM   HASTEN   PRISTINE
CONFISCATE   DAWDLE
EPIC

Health Cause & Effect

Score: _____

Date: _____

Staying healthy means taking care of your body so you can grow strong and feel good. Eating lots of fruits and vegetables is a great start because they're full of vitamins that help your body fight off sickness. It's also import to drink plenty of water every day to keep hydrated. Try to choose snacks like nuts or yogurt instead of too muc candy or chips, which can make you feel sluggish.

Being active is another key part of staying healthy. Activities like running, jumping rope, or playing sports with friends are not only fun but also keep your heart and muscles strong. Even walking your dog or dancing in your room counts as being active!

Getting enough sleep each night is crucial too because it helps your body and brain rest and recharge. Try to stick to a regular bedtime and limit screen time before bed to help you fall asleep easier.

Lastly, always remember to wash your hands regularly to keep germs away, especially before eating. Making these healthy choices every day will help you feel your best and do well in school and play!

#		Cause	Effect
1	☐	Smoking	Extreme weather events
2	☐	Deforestation	Loss of biodiversity
3	☐	High sugar intake	Diabetes
4	☐	Excessive alcohol consumption	Lung cancer
5	☐	Air pollution	Heart disease
6	☐	Sedentary lifestyle	Mental health issues
7	☐	Climate change	Respiratory diseases
8	☐	Poor diet	Obesity
9	☐	Stress	Liver disease
10	☐	Neglect	Child development problems

Find the Change, Price, or Amount Paid

en you buy something, the price is how much it costs. The amount paid is the money you give to the cashier. If you pay e than the price, the cashier gives you back the extra money, called the change. To find the change, subtract the price from amount you paid. It's like if you have $10, buy something for $7, and get $3 back as change!

ose the correct answer for each question below. Need help? Try Google.

1. If you buy a book for $15 and pay with a $20 bill, how much change will you receive?
   a. $10
   b. $5
   c. $3

2. You purchased a shirt for $25 and gave the cashier $30. What is the amount of change you should get back?
   a. $10
   b. $5
   c. $2

3. A movie ticket costs $12. If you pay $20, how much change will you receive?
   a. $8
   b. $7
   c. $5

4. You ordered a pizza for $18 and paid with a $50 bill. What is your change?
   a. $28
   b. $25
   c. $32

5. If a sandwich costs $9 and you pay with a $10 bill, how much change do you get?
   a. $3
   b. $2
   c. $1

6. You buy a coffee for $4.50 and give the cashier $5. What is the change?
   a. $0.50
   b. $0.25
   c. $1

7. A video game costs $60. If you pay $100, how much change will you receive?
   a. $30
   b. $50
   c. $40

8. You buy a dress for $45 and pay with a $100 bill. How much change do you get back?
   a. $60
   b. $55
   c. $50

9. If a bag of groceries costs $75 and you pay with a $100 bill, what is your change?
   a. $20
   b. $30
   c. $25

10. You pay $18 for a meal and give the waiter a $20 bill. How much is your change?
    a. $3
    b. $1
    c. $2

Test Your Knowledge

Part 1: Parts of Speech

1. A noun is a word that describes an action or a state of being.

True	False

2. Which of the following is an adjective?

A. Run	B. Quickly	C. Blue

3. Identify the verb in this sentence: "The cat slept on the warm, sunny windowsill."

Part 2: Verb Tenses

4. The past perfect tense describes an action that will happen in the future.

True	False

5. What is the present progressive tense of the verb "to run"?

6. Fill in the blank with the correct form of the verb "to go": "By the time we arrived at the cinema, the movie _____ already started."

Part 3: Sentence Structure

7. A compound sentence contains two or more independent clauses and one or more dependent clauses.

True	False

8. Identify the subject in this sentence: "In the garden, the beautiful flowers bloom brightly."

9. Write a complex sentence using the word "although."

Part 4: Punctuation

10. A semicolon can be used to connect two closely related independent clauses.

True	False

11. Which of the following sentences is punctuated correctly? A. "Let's eat grandma!" B. "Let's eat, grandma!"

12. Correct the punctuation in this sentence: "She said I'm sorry for your loss."

Earth Science Crossword

Cross

. supercontinent that scientists believe existed years ago

. large sections of the Earth's crust that slowly move

. elevation difference between different areas of a region

. surface where plants grow

. opening in the Earth's crust where molten rock erupts

Down

1. formed from great heat and pressure inside the Earth's crust

2. is a solid substance that occurs naturally

3. geological landform that rises significantly above the surrounding land

4. The rising and falling of sea levels

8. place where the Earth's crust is being pulled apart

9. Rocks formed from years of sediment

11. the physical features of an area of land

METAMORPHIC ROCK
MOUNTAIN   SOIL
PANGEA   TECTONIC
PLATES   VOLCANO
SEDIMENTARY ROCK
MINERAL   RELIEF   RIFT
TOPOGRAPHY   OCEAN
TIDE

The First Thanksgiving

Score_____

Date:_____

The First Thanksgiving was a feast in 1621 where the Pilgrims and the Wampanoag Native Americans celebrated a successful harvest together. It marked a time of cooperation and sharing between the two groups. This event is considered the beginning of the Thanksgiving tradition in the United States.

Need help? Try Google or your favorite search engine.

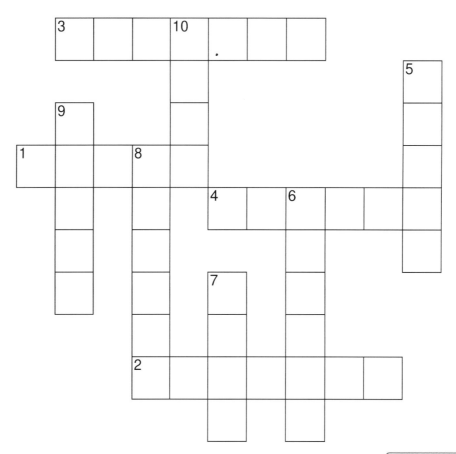

Across

1. A large meal with many different foods.
2. The gathering of ripe crops from the fields.
3. One of the English settlers who celebrated the First Thanksgiving.
4. A person originally from a particular place, like the Wampanoag.

Down

5. The leader of a Native American tribe.
6. A large bird often eaten at Thanksgiving meals.
7. A type of grain that was an important food for both Pilgrims and Native Americans.
8. A vegetable that was part of the First Thanksgiving feast.
9. A time without conflict or war, like when the Pilgrims and Wampanoag came together.
10. Something given to someone without expecting anything in return, symbolizing sharing and kindness.

CHIEF   PEACE   PILGRIM
GIFT   CORN   HARVEST
TURKEY   FEAST   NATIVE
SQUASH

Today Is Spelling Day!

:le the correct spelling word then write it in cursive on the line provided.

	A	B	C	D
1. _____	bandadge	bandadje	bandage	bandaje
2. _____	chest	chesct	chesst	chast
3. _____	dripht	drripht	drrift	drift
4. _____	dul	dull	voll	dol
5. _____	dussk	dusck	dossk	dusk
6. _____	sttratch	sttretch	stretch	stratch
7. _____	flock	flok	fllock	fllok
8. _____	ffnd	funo	fond	fpnd
9. _____	meassure	maessure	maesure	measure
10. _____	cacttos	cactos	cacttus	cactus
11. _____	scrap	scrrap	scrrep	screp
12. _____	shift	shifft	shiphft	shipht
13. _____	smasch	smesh	smash	smassh
14. _____	switch	swyttch	swytch	swittch
15. _____	sweptt	swept	swapt	swaptt
16. _____	thrraet	thrreat	threat	thraet
17. _____	tymid	tymwd	timir	timid
18. _____	plliad	plaid	pllaid	pliad
19. _____	trrust	trust	trost	trrost
20. _____	twisct	twyst	twisst	twist

Coronavirus Outbreak Pandemic

First, read over the entire passage(s). Then go back and fill in the blanks. You can skip the blanks you're unsui about and come back to them later.

strain	bombarded	physician	elderly	cells
symptoms	nose	China	system	lathering

If you've been around adults, you've probably heard a lot of talk about "coronavirus." This virus has evolved int new _____ that is spreading throughout the world. It is called a coronavirus because the Latin wc "corona" means "crown." Additionally, the virus appears to be wearing a spiky crown.

Generally, it causes coughing, fatigue, and a fever. However, it can be extremely dangerous for the _____ and those with other medical conditions. COVID-19 is the name of the virus that causes th disease.

In December 2019, Wuhan, a city in _____, was the first place to discover the virus. However, we believe the virus originated in bats. It then hopped into another type of animal, passing it on to humans. Nobod knows for sure what this mysterious animal was, but some believe it was a pangolin, a scaly animal that feeds ants.

The virus enters _____ via a unique "door" located on the exterior of human cells. Additionally, th new coronavirus requires a "key" to enter cells. The coronavirus, in this case, has a unique "spike" on its surfac that it uses as a key to open the door.

Viruses cause illness by either killing human cells or impairing their function. As previously stated, the new coronavirus enters cells via a unique door. These unique entry points are located on cells in the _____ and lungs. If the virus multiplies too rapidly in the lungs, breathing can be difficult. This is referred to as pneumonia.

Fortunately, your body is equipped with an army to combat germs like coronavirus. It is referred to as the immu _____. When a virus enters your body, it is attacked by your immune system. You know how whe 're sick, you can develop a fever, a headache, or a runny nose? That is the result of the immune system, and beneficial! These unpleasant symptoms indicate that your body is battling the virus.

e majority of people who contract COVID-19 experience only mild _____ such as a cough, fever, unny nose. Doctors are unsure why some people become extremely ill. Certain individuals' immune systems y not be strong enough. Other people's immune systems may be overly aggressive, causing damage to their n cells. Both of these factors have the potential to make people sicker.

ere is a special test to determine whether or not you have COVID-19. Inform your parents if you become ill. y will contact your _____ to decide whether or not you require the test. It's similar to a flu test; y insert a Q-tip into your nose and examine your snot for the presence of the virus. The results are returned following day.

ce inside cells, the virus multiplies rapidly. These virus copies replicate outside of cells and then infect other s. When our normal cells are _____ with so many virus particles, they lose their ability to ction properly... and we become ill.

washing your hands, you can help prevent the spread of the virus. This involves _____ up with p and rubbing your hands together to thoroughly clean all of your fingers, under the fingernails, and between fingers. You can sing the ABCs or create a new tune lasting approximately 20 seconds.

ditionally, remember to cough or sneeze into your elbow (as if you were a vampire!) and stay home if you are k.

Put Decimal Numbers in Order

Putting decimal numbers in order means arranging them from smallest to largest, or the other way around. First look at the numbers to the left of the decimal point; the smaller that number, the smaller the whole decimal. If those numbers are the same, then look at the digits right after the decimal point. Compare each digit in order u you find a difference—the smallest digit means the smallest decimal. Line up the decimals in order based on w you find, and you'll have them neatly arranged!

Choose the correct answer for each question below. Need more help? Try Google.

1. Which of the following decimal numbers is the largest?
   - a. 4.7
   - b. 4.6
   - c. 4.5

2. Put the following numbers in order from smalle to largest: 2.3, 2.1, 2.5
   - a. 2.5, 2.3, 2.1
   - b. 2.3, 2.5, 2.1
   - c. 2.1, 2.3, 2.5

3. Which of these numbers is the smallest?
   - a. 3.04
   - b. 3.14
   - c. 3.4

4. Arrange the following in ascending order: 1.25 1.5, 1.1
   - a. 1.1, 1.25, 1.5
   - b. 1.25, 1.1, 1.5
   - c. 1.5, 1.25, 1.1

5. Which decimal is greater than 0.75?
   - a. 0.6
   - b. 0.8
   - c. 0.7

6. Order these decimals from largest to smallest: 0.5, 0.05, 0.55
   - a. 0.5, 0.55, 0.05
   - b. 0.55, 0.5, 0.05
   - o. 0.06, 0.6, 0.66

7. Which number is smaller than 0.3?
   - a. 0.4
   - b. 0.25
   - c. 0.35

8. Put these numbers in order from largest to smallest: 5.1, 5.01, 5.001
   - a. 5.01, 5.1, 5.001
   - b. 5.001, 5.01, 5.1
   - c. 5.1, 5.01, 5.001

9. Which decimal is equal to 1.5?
   - a. 1.50
   - b. 1.5
   - c. 1.55

10. Arrange these decimals in ascending order: 0.9 0.99, 0.8
    - a. 0.99, 0.9, 0.8
    - b. 0.9, 0.8, 0.99
    - c. 0.8, 0.9, 0.99

Alphabetize and Define

meter	1. _____
irony	2. _____
personification	3. _____
denotation	4. _____
onomatopoeia	5. _____
alliteration	6. _____
rhyme	7. _____
metaphor	
theme	8. _____
symbolism	9. _____
repetition	10. _____
simile	11. _____
stanza	12. _____
connotation	13. _____
imagery	14. _____
	15. _____

ter putting the words in alphabetical order, choose 5 and write a definition in the space provided.

_____

_____

_____

Predicting Weather

Score: _____

Date: _____

Sentence Building: Unscramble the sentences!

(Use a separate sheet of paper to write out sentences if needed.)

1. _____

to · technologies · advanced · of · the · meteorology, · and · involves · weather, · atmospheric · as · Predicting · conditions. · also · forecast · known · scientific · use · principles

2. _____

sources, · stations, · current · radar · to · systems, · understand · including · imagery, · patterns · various · analyze · data · from · and · Meteorologists · weather · weather · satellite

3. _____

behavior, · future · make · They · to · computer · them · about · simulate · the · weather · utilize · predictions · atmosphere's · allowing · models · events. · that

4. _____

These · climate · precipitation, · long-term · like · seasonal · outlooks · forecasts, · short-term · range · trends. · can · as · from · such · and · temperatures · daily · predictions

5. _____

pressure · play · as · wind · Factors · features · and · all · crucial · shaping · patterns, · systems, · in · roles · geographic · forecasts. · weather · such · humidity,

6. _____

informed · to · severe · and · technology · advances, · continues · the · As · decisions. · communities · of · weather · helping · predictions · prepare · improve, · for · making · weather · accuracy

The Transcontinental Railroad

uring this exercise, fill in the blanks with the correct word. Need help? Try Google or your favorite search engine.

coasts	constructed	Tunnel	continent	Steam
Union	vehicle	Bridge	Golden	Railroad
Journey	Central	Tracks	rails	Transport

1. _____ - A track with rails on which trains run.

2. Transcontinental - Stretching across a _____.

3. Train - A _____ that runs on tracks and carries people or goods.

4. _____ - The rails on which a train travels.

5. _____ Spike - The final spike driven into the railroad to complete it.

6. Builders - People who _____ the railroad.

7. _____ - A structure built to allow the train to cross over rivers or valleys.

8. _____ - A passage built through mountains for the train to pass.

9. Laying Tracks - The process of placing the _____ on the ground.

10. _____ - What powered the early trains.

11. _____ Pacific - One of the companies that built the railroad from the east.

12. _____ Pacific - The company that built the railroad from the west.

13. Connection - Bringing the two _____ together with the railroad.

14. _____ - Moving people or goods from one place to another.

15. _____ - Traveling from one place to another, often made easier by the railroad.

Math Terms Matching

Score: _____

Date: _____

Match each math term to the correct meaning.

1	[ ]	Rectangle
2	[ ]	Negative Number
3	[ ]	Triangle
4	[ ]	X
5	[ ]	X-Axis
6	[ ]	Weight
7	[ ]	Like Fractions
8	[ ]	Like Terms
9	[ ]	Mode
10	[ ]	Midpoint
11	[ ]	Line
12	[ ]	Numerator
13	[ ]	Octagon
14	[ ]	Logic
15	[ ]	Outcome
16	[ ]	Polynomial
17	[ ]	Quotient
18	[ ]	Proper Fraction

A parallelogram with four right angles.

The measure of how heavy something is.

A three-sided polygon.

The Roman numeral for 10.

A straight infinite path joining an infinite number of points in both directions.

The _____ is a list of numbers are the values that occur most frequently.

A number less than zero.

A point that is exactly halfway between two locations.

The top number in a fraction.

The sum of two or more monomials.

_____ with the same variable and same exponents/powers.

The solution to a division problem.

Fractions with the same denominator.

Sound reasoning and the formal laws of reasoning.

Used in probability to refer to the result of an event.

The horizontal axis in a coordinate plane.

A polygon with eight sides.

A fraction whose denominator is greater than its numerator.

SUPERLATIVE ADJECTIVES

Date: _____

superlative adjective is a comparative adjective that describes something as being of the highest degree or treme. When comparing three or more people or things, we use superlative adjectives. Superlative adjectives ically end in 'est'. Examples of superlative adjectives include the words biggest and fastest.

scramble Word Tip: Try solving the easy words first, and then go back and answer the more difficult ones.

prettiest	hottest	crowded	friendliest	biggest	smallest
saddest	best	worst	tallest	shortest	longest
fattest	newest	heaviest	nicest	beautiful	expensive
cheapest	comfortable	youngest	largest		

peehtsac _ h _ a _ _ _ _

talresg _ _ _ _ e s _

ntogels _ o n _ _ _ _

wsenet n e _ _ _ _

icetns n _ _ _ s _

tstosreh _ _ _ r _ _ _ t

samlsetl _ _ _ _ l _ _ t

lstteal _ a _ _ e _ _

goysunte _ _ _ n _ _ s _

). tggsbie _ _ _ g _ s _

1. eftastt _ _ t _ _ _ t

12. ttoesht h _ _ _ e _ _

13. adstdes _ _ d _ _ s _

14. filtaubeu _ _ a _ _ _ _ _ l

15. ctlefarbmoo _ _ _ _ _ r _ a b _ _

16. ddrwoce _ _ _ _ _ e d

17. enpsvxeei e _ _ _ n _ _ _ _ _

18. esdeirfiltn _ r _ _ _ _ l _ _ s _

19. hitvseea h _ _ _ _ _ _ t

20. espttriet _ r _ _ _ i _ _ _

21. bets _ _ s _

22. wrsot _ _ _ s _

Introduction to Atoms

During this exercise, fill in the blanks with the correct word. Need help? Try Google or your favorite search engine.

Electrons	chemical	three	destroyed	nucleus
negative	smell	Neutrons	empty	molecules
Protons	tiny	properties	matter	microscopes

1. Atoms are the _____ building blocks that make up everything around us, from the air we breathe to the food we ea

2. An atom is the smallest unit of matter that retains the _____ of an element, like gold or oxygen.

3. Atoms are tiny particles that are so small you can't see them with your eyes, only through special

   _____.

4. Atoms are the basic units that make up all the _____ elements on the periodic table, like hydrogen and helium.

5. An atom is made up of _____ main parts.

6. The center of an atom, called the _____, contains protons and neutrons.

7. _____ are tiny particles that orbit around the nucleus, much like planets orbiting the sun.

8. _____, found in the nucleus, have a positive electrical charge

9. Electrons, which move around the nucleus, have a _____ electrical charge

10. _____, also in the nucleus, have no electrical charge; they are neutral.

11. Everything you can touch, see, _____, or taste is made of atoms joined together.

12. Atoms can join together to form _____, which are groups of atoms bonded together.

13. Atoms can change forms but cannot be created or _____ in ordinary chemical reactions.

14. Most of an atom is _____ space, with a tiny dense nucleus in the center and electrons zooming around it.

15. Even though we can't see atoms, they are incredibly powerful and essential for the structure and function of all

    _____.

The New Deal

st, read all the way through. After that, go back and fill in the blanks. You can skip the blanks you're unsure about and finish them
er.

harvests	public	economic	farmers	country's
crisis	President	Social	government	Civilian

ie New Deal was a series of programs and policies introduced by _____ Franklin D.
oosevelt to help the United States recover from the Great Depression. The Great Depression was a
vere economic _____ that began in 1929 and caused widespread unemployment,
verty, and suffering.

hen Franklin D. Roosevelt became President in 1933, he promised to take action and help the
untry get back on its feet. The New Deal included many different programs aimed at providing jobs,
pporting _____, and helping people in need.

ie of the key parts of the New Deal was the creation of _____ works projects. These
ere large construction projects that provided jobs for millions of Americans. People built roads,
idges, schools, and parks. These projects not only gave people work but also improved the
_____ infrastructure.

iother important part of the New Deal was the _____ Security Act. This program
ovided financial support to elderly people, the disabled, and unemployed workers. It helped ensure
at people had some money to live on even if they couldn't work.

ie New Deal also included programs to help farmers. Many farmers were struggling because of low
op prices and poor _____. The government offered loans and subsidies to help them
ep their farms running and support their families.

dditionally, the New Deal established agencies like the _____ Conservation Corps
CC) and the Works Progress Administration (WPA). The CCC put young men to work in national
arks and forests, planting trees and building trails. The WPA hired artists, writers, and musicians to
eate public art and perform in communities.

ie New Deal didn't solve all the problems of the Great Depression, but it provided hope and relief to
any Americans. It showed that the _____ could take action to help people in times of
eed. President Roosevelt's New Deal left a lasting impact on the country and laid the foundation for
ture social and _____ programs.

Numbers Vocabulary: Math, Time, & Money Study Guide

Score: _____

Date: _____

1	☐	Add	a number in a system first used in ancient Rome that uses combinations of the letters I, V, X, L, C, D, and M to represent numbers ≠ Arabic numeral
2	☐	ATM	the money that you get back when you have paid for something with more money than it costs: money in the form of coins, not paper money (noun); to become different, or to make something become different: to take off your clothes and put on different ones (verb)
3	☐	Borrow	to put something with something else or with a group of other things: to increase the amount or cost of something: if you add numbers or amounts together, you calculate their total≠ subtract
4	☐	Cardinal Number	the time during the summer when clocks are one hour ahead of standard time: daylight savings
5	☐	Cash	abbreviation for automated teller machine: a machine outside a bank that you use to get money from your account
6	☐	Change	a plastic card with your signature on it, that resembles a credit card, but functions like a check and through which payments for purchases or services are made electronically to pay for things, the money is taken directly from your bank account
7	☐	Check	to let someone borrow money or something that belongs to you for a short time: if a bank or financial institution lends money, it lets someone have it on condition that they pay it back later, often gradually, with an additional amount as interest ≠borrow
8	☐	Clockwise	in the same direction as the hands of a clock move ≠ counterclockwise
9	☐	Counterclockwise	having the same value, purpose, job etc. as a person or thing of a different kind (adj.): something that has the same value, purpose, job etc. as something else; something that is equal in value, amount, quality etc. to something else (noun)
10	☐	Daylight Saving Time	a piece of paper that you are given which shows that you have paid for something: when someone receives something
11	☐	Debit Card	the same in size, number, amount, value etc. as something else: equivalent: having the same rights, opportunities etc. as everyone else, whatever your race, religion, or sex
12	☐	Deposit	to take a number or an amount from a larger number or amount: deduct, minus

Divide	☐	to find the size, length, or amount of something, using standard units such as inches, meters etc.: to judge the importance, value, or true nature of something: if a piece of equipment measures something, it shows or records a particular kind of measurement	M
Equal	☐	to use something, often money, that belongs to someone else and that you must give back to them later: to take or copy someone's ideas, words etc and use them in your own work, language etc.≠lend, loan	N
Equivalent	☐	the length, height etc. of something: the act of measuring something	O
Fraction	☐	a printed piece of paper that you write an amount of money on, sign, and use instead of money to pay for things (noun); to do something in order to find out whether something really is correct, true, or in good condition: to make a mark (✓) next to an answer, something on a list etc. to show you have chosen it, that it is correct, or that you have dealt with it (verb)	P
Lend	☐	a very small amount of something: a part of a whole number in mathematics, such as ½ or ¾	Q
Measure	☐	one of the 24 areas that the world is divided into, each of which has its own time	R
Measurement	☐	if something divides, or if you divide it, it separates into two or more parts: to keep two areas separate from each other: to calculate how many times one number contains a smaller number: to make people disagree so that they form groups with different opinions	S
Ordinal Number	☐	a part of the cost of something you are buying that you pay some time before you pay the rest of it: money that you pay when you rent something such as an apartment or car, which will be given back if you do not damage it: an amount of money that is paid into a bank account ≠ withdrawal (noun); to put money or something valuable in a bank or other place where it will be safe: to put something down in a particular place (verb)	T
Receipt	☐	money in the form of coins or notes rather than checks, credit cards etc.: money (noun); to exchange a check etc. for cash (verb)	U
Roman Numeral	☐	in the opposite direction to the way in which the hands of a clock move around: anticlockwise ≠ counterclockwise	V
Subtract	☐	a number such as 1, 2, or 3, that shows how many of something there are, but not what order they are in ≠ Ordinal Number	W
Time Zone	☐	one of the numbers such as first, second, third etc. which show the order of things ≠ Cardinal Number	X
Withdraw	☐	to take money out of a bank account: to stop taking part in an activity, belonging to an organization etc., or to make someone do this	Y

It's Sentence Building Day!

Score: _____

Date: _____

Practice *sentence* building. *Unscramble* the words to form a complete sentence.

1. _____

   it · around · plant · a · When · kills · volcano · life · erupts · the · it.

2. _____

   I · banana · one · eat · every · day.

3. _____

   or · travel. · locomotion · term · movement · means · The

4. _____

   says · learn. · teacher · repetition · help · us · will · Our

5. _____

   about? · What · commotion · is · all · the

6. _____

   have · away. · car · taken · good · maintain · my · will · grades · I · be · to · or

7. _____

   person's · about · monkey · The · curious · camera. · was · the

8. _____

   becoming · should · am · drink · so · dehydrated · I · know · water. · I · I

9. _____

   your · will · I · now. · all · confiscate · candy · of

10. _____

    to · countries' · trying · Our · best · are · do · the · what's · governments · for · people.

11. _____

    semiprecious · is · Amethyst · a · stone.

Fascinating Stars

st, read all the way through. After that, go back and fill in the blanks. You can skip the blanks you're unsure about and finish them
er.

temperature	patterns	temperatures	balls	Earth
outer	explode	hydrogen	atmosphere	nebulae

ırs are fascinating, twinkling objects in the night sky. They are giant _____ of glowing gas, mostly hydrogen and helium,
d they produce light and heat through a process called nuclear fusion.

w Stars are Born

ırs are born in huge clouds of gas and dust called _____. When parts of these clouds collapse under their own gravity,
ey heat up and start to glow, forming a new star. This process can take millions of years!

pes of Stars

ırs come in different sizes, colors, and _____. Here are a few types:

Red Dwarfs: These are small and cool stars. They are the most common type of star in the universe and can live for trillions of years.
Yellow Dwarfs: Our Sun is a yellow dwarf. These stars are medium-sized and have a moderate temperature. They can live for about
 billion years.
Blue Giants: These are large and very hot stars. They are blue because they burn at very high temperatures. Blue giants have
orter lifespans, often only a few million years.
Supergiants: Even bigger than blue giants, supergiants are some of the largest stars in the universe. They can _____
massive supernovae at the end of their lives.

e Life Cycle of a Star

Formation: Stars begin their life in a nebula.
Main Sequence: This is the longest stage of a star's life where it burns _____ into helium. Our Sun is currently in this
ıge.
Red Giant or Supergiant: When stars exhaust their hydrogen, they expand and cool down to become red giants or supergiants.
End of Life: Stars end their lives differently depending on their size. Smaller stars may shed their _____ layers and
ıve behind a white dwarf. Larger stars might explode in a supernova, leaving behind a neutron star or a black hole.

ınstellations

ırs often appear to form _____ in the sky, called constellations. Ancient people named these patterns after animals,
ıthological characters, and objects. For example, Orion is a famous constellation that looks like a hunter.

ın Facts

Distances: Stars are very far away from us. The closest star to _____, other than the Sun, is Proxima Centauri, which is
ıout 4.24 light-years away.
winkling: Stars appear to twinkle because of the Earth's _____. As the light from stars passes through different layers
 air, it bends and makes the stars seem to flicker.
Star Colors: A star's color tells us its _____. Blue stars are hot, while red stars are cooler.

ırs are incredible, and studying them helps us learn more about the universe and our place in it. Next time you look at the night sky,
ınk about the amazing journeys of these distant suns!

Nullification Crisis

During this exercise, you will fill in the blanks with the correct word to match the definitions or clues.

development	crisis	President	defying	argued
threats	benefiting	federal	conflict	slavery
outbreak	enforce	Latin	Congress	Vice

1. The Nullification Crisis was a political _____ in the United States that occurred between 1832 and 1833.

2. It was centered around the issue of states' rights versus _____ rights, particularly regarding the power to nullify or cancel federal laws.

3. The _____ began when South Carolina declared that two federal tariffs (taxes on imported goods), passed in 1828 and 1832, were unconstitutional and, therefore, did not have to be obeyed within their state's borders.

4. These tariffs, known as the "Tariffs of Abominations," were seen as _____ the industrial North at th expense of the agricultural South.

5. South Carolina, led by Senator John C. Calhoun, _____ that states should have the right to nullify federal law they believed those laws were unconstitutional.

6. The Nullification Crisis was one of the earliest major _____ to the unity of the United States and foreshadowed the later Civil War.

7. In response to South Carolina's nullification act, _____ Andrew Jackson declared it to be treasonous.

8. Jackson, a firm believer in the federal government's supremacy over the states, signed the Force Bill into law in 1833, giving him the power to use military force to _____ federal laws in South Carolina.

9. The crisis was eventually resolved when _____ passed a compromise bill known as the Compromise Ta of 1833, which gradually lowered the tariffs.

10. John C. Calhoun was _____ President under Andrew Jackson but resigned due to their differing views during the crisis.

11. The Nullification Crisis highlighted the growing tensions between the North and South over issues of states' rights and _____ .

12. The crisis was a key moment in the _____ of the concept of secession or the idea that a state could choose to leave the Union.

13. The term "nullification" comes from the _____ word "nullus," which means "none. " It refers to the idea of making something legally null and void.

14. The crisis showed the potential dangers of a single state _____ federal law, setting the stage for future conflicts.

15. Despite the resolution of the crisis, the issues of states' rights and federal authority continued to be contentious topics American politics, eventually contributing to the _____ of the Civil War.

Look It Up! Pop Quiz

arn some basic vocabulary words that you will come across again and again in the course of your studies in algebra. By knowing the definitions
most algebra words, you will be able to construct and solve algebra problems much more easily.

d the answer to the questions below by *looking up each word. (The wording can be tricky. Take your time.)*

1. improper fraction

    a. a fraction that the denominator is equal to the numerator

    b. a fraction in which the numerator is greater than the denominator, is always 1 or greater .

2. equivalent fraction

    a. a fraction that has a DIFFERENT value as a given fraction

    b. a fraction that has the SAME value as a given fraction

3. simplest form of fraction

    a. an equivalent fraction for which the only common factor of the numerator and denominator is 1

    b. an equivalent fraction for which the only least factor of the denominator is -1

4. mixed number

    a. the sum of a whole number and a proper fraction

    b. the sum of a variable and a fraction

5. reciprocal

    a. a number that can be divided by another number to make 10

    b. a number that can be multiplied by another number to make 1

6. percent

    a. a percentage that compares a number to 0.1

    b. a ratio that compares a number to 100

7. sequence

    a. a set of addition numbers that follow a operation

    b. a set of numbers that follow a pattern

8. arithmetic sequence

    a. a sequence where EACH term is found by adding or subtracting the exact same number to the previous term

    b. a sequence where NO term is found by multiplying the exact same number to the previous term

9. geometric sequence

    a. a sequence where each term is found by multiplying or dividing by the exact same number to the previous term

    b. a sequence where each term is solved by adding or dividing by a different number to the previous term

10. order of operations

    a. the procedure to follow when simplifying a numerical expression

    b. the procedure to follow when adding any fraction by 100

11. variable expression

    a. a mathematical phrase that contains variables, numbers, and operation symbols

    b. a mathematical phrase that contains numbers and operation symbols

12. absolute value

    a. the distance a number is from zero on the number line

    b. the range a number is from one on the number line

13. integers

    a. a set of numbers that includes whole numbers and their opposites

    b. a set of numbers that includes equal numbers and their difference

14. x-axis

    a. the horizontal number line that, together with the y-axis, establishes the coordinate plane

    b. the vertical number line that, together with the y-axis, establishes the coordinate plane

15. y-axis

   a. the vertical number line that, together with the x-axis, establishes the coordinate plane

   b. the horizontal number line that, together with the x-axis, establishes the coordinate plane

16. coordinate plane

   a. plane formed by one number line (the horizontal y-axis and the vertical x-axis) intersecting at their -1 points

   b. plane formed by two number lines (the horizontal x-axis and the vertical y-axis) intersecting at their zero points

17. quadrant

   a. one of two sections on the four plane formed by the intersection of the x-axis

   b. one of four sections on the coordinate plane formed by the intersection of the x-axis and the y-axis

18. ordered pair

   a. a pair of numbers that gives the location of a point in the coordinate plane. Also known as the "coordinate" of a point.

   b. a pair of equal numbers that gives the range of a po in the axis plane. Also known as the "y-axis" of a point.

19. x-coordinate

   a. the number that indicates the position of a point to the left or right of the y-axis

   b. the number that indicates the range of a point to the left ONLY of the y-axis

20. y-coordinate

   a. the number that indicates the position of a point abo or below the x-axis

   b. the number that indicates the value of a point only above the x-axis

21. inverse operations

   a. operations that equals to each other

   b. operations that undo each other

22. inequality

   a. a math sentence that uses a letter (x or y) to indicate that the left and right sides of the sentence hold values that are different

   b. a math sentence that uses a symbol ($<, >, \leq, \geq, \neq$) to indicate that the left and right sides of the sentence hold values that are different

23. perimeter

   a. the distance around the outside of a figure

   b. the distance around the inside of a figure

24. circumference

   a. the distance around a circle

   b. the range around a square

25. area

   a. the number of square units inside a 2-dimensional figure

   b. the number of circle units inside a 3-dimensional figure

26. volume

   a. the number of cubic units inside a 3-dimensional figure

   b. the number of cubic squared units inside a 2-dimensional figure

27. radius

   a. a line segment that runs from the middle of the circle to end of the circle

   b. a line segment that runs from the center of the circle to somewhere on the circle

28. chord

   a. a line segment that runs from somewhere on the circ to another place on the circle

   b. a circle distance that runs from somewhere on the fa left to another place on the circle

29. diameter

   a. a chord that passes through the center of the circle

   b. a thin line that passes through the end of the circle

30. mean

   a. the sum of the data items added by the number of data items minus 2

   b. the sum of the data items divided by the number of data items

31. median

   a. the first data item found after sorting the data items in descending order

   b. the middle data item found after sorting the data items in ascending order

32. mode

   a. the data item that occurs most often

   b. the data item that occurs less than two times

33. range

    a. the difference between the highest and the lowest data item

    b. the difference between the middle number and the lowest number item

35. ratio

    a. a comparison of two quantities by multiplication

    b. a comparison of two quantities by division

37. proportion

    a. a statement (ratio) showing five or more ratios to be equal

    b. a statement (equation) showing two ratios to be equal

39. probability

    a. a ratio that explains the likelihood of the distance and miles between to places

    b. a ratio that explains the likelihood of an event

41. experimental probability

    a. the ratio of the number of times by 2 when an event occurs to the number of times times 2 an experiment is done (based on real experimental data).

    b. the ratio of the number of times an event occurs to the number of times an experiment is done (based on real experimental data).

43. term

    a. a number, a variable, or probability of an equal number and a variable(s)

    b. a number, a variable, or product of a number and a variable(s)

45. Coefficient

    a. a number that divides a variable

    b. a number that multiplies a variable

34. outlier

    a. a data item that is much higher or much lower than all the other data items

    b. a data item that is much lower or less than all the other data items

36. rate

    a. a ratio that has equal quantities measured in the same units

    b. a ratio that compares quantities measured in different units

38. outcomes

    a. possible results of action

    b. possible answer when two numbers are the same

40. theoretical probability

    a. the probability of the highest favorable number of possible outcomes (based on what is not expected to occur).

    b. the ratio of the number of favorable outcomes to the number of possible outcomes (based on what is expected to occur).

42. distributive property

    a. a way to simplify an expression that contains a equal like term being added by a group of terms.

    b. a way to simplify an expression that contains a single term being multiplied by a group of terms.

44. Constant

    a. a term with no variable part (i.e. a number)

    b. a term with no variable + y part (i.e. 4+y)

Are vs. Our

Depending on your exact pronunciation, it can sometimes be difficult for someone to tell whether you're saying "are" or "our."

Are is used in the English simple present tense. It shows that something exists. Are is also a helping verb. Are pronounced like "arrr".

Our is the possessive form of we. The proper pronunciation of the word is two syllables, "oww-er".

Circle the correct answer.

1. [Are / Our] school holiday is two weeks long.

2. You [are / our] very good at spelling.

3. [Our / Are] we going to the picnic?

4. As a school, we do [are / our] best to meet the needs of every student.

5. We [our / are] driving to visit a friend.

6. We went to the dog shelter and picked out [are / our] new dog together.

7. We [are / our] going to win the band contest this year.

8. After the terrible breakup, he realized that there [our / are] other fish in the sea.

9. When the homeowners opened the door, they exclaimed, "Welcome to [are / our] house!"

10. Since everyone shared it, the family called it ["our / are] car."

11. The Smiths [our / are] very wealthy people.

12. There [our / are] sixty minutes in an hour.

13. [Our / We] school holiday is two weeks long.

Atoms in Space

st, read all the way through. After that, go back and fill in the blanks. You can skip the blanks you're unsure about and finish them
er.

atoms	gas	neutrons	iron	Stars
nuclear	vacuum	nucleus	nebulae	universe

agine looking up at the night sky and seeing all those twinkling stars. Did you know that everything you see up there, from stars to
nets, is made of tiny particles called _____? Atoms are the building blocks of everything in the universe, including
ace itself!

oms are incredibly small. In fact, they are so tiny that millions of them can fit on the tip of a pin! Each atom is made up of a
_____, which has protons and _____, and electrons that zoom around the nucleus like planets orbiting the
n.

space, atoms combine to form all sorts of amazing things. _____, for example, are giant balls of gas made primarily of
drogen and helium atoms. These atoms collide and fuse together in a process called _____ fusion, which releases a
mendous amount of energy and makes the stars shine brightly.

nets, moons, and asteroids are also made of atoms. The Earth, for instance, is composed of various elements like oxygen, silicon,
d _____, each made of their own unique atoms. These atoms bond together to form rocks, water, air, and everything
e that makes up our planet.

en the vast emptiness of space, known as the _____, isn't completely empty. It contains sparse atoms and subatomic
rticles floating around. Sometimes, clouds of _____ and dust in space, called _____, are made of these
oms. These nebulae can eventually come together to form new stars and planets.

ientists study atoms in space to learn more about the _____. By understanding how atoms interact and form different
uctures, we can discover the secrets of stars, galaxies, and even the origins of life itself.

, whenever you gaze at the stars, remember that those distant lights are made of the same tiny atoms that make up everything here
Earth. The universe is a vast, atom-filled playground waiting to be explored!

Battle of Yorktown

First, read all the way through. After that, go back and fill in the blanks. You can skip the blanks you're unsure about and finish them later.

morale	clever	surrender	escape	end
General	siege	consequences	battlefield	French

Long, long ago, in a land that's now our very own backyard, a battle took place that would change the course of history forever. This battle was known as the Battle of Yorktown, and it marked the _____ of a fierce and fiery period known as the American Revolution.

Imagine a giant game of chess, but instead of playing on a small board, the players used the entire city of Yorktown as their _____. The British, led by General Lord Cornwallis, were the red pieces, and the Americans, along with their French allies, were the blue pieces. The generals moved their soldiers like chess pieces, each one trying to outsmart the other.

The American general, George Washington, was like a clever fox. He had a secret weapon - his French friend, _____ Rochambeau. Together, they hatched a plan as sly as a fox sneaking into a chicken coop. They decided to surround Yorktown, cutting off any chance for the British soldiers to _____ or get more supplies. It was like trapping a group of ants inside a circle drawn with chalk.

The _____ of Yorktown lasted for several weeks. Can you imagine being stuck in your school for weeks with no new food supplies coming in? That's how it was for the British soldiers. Slowly but surely, like a cookie jar being emptied bit by bit, their strength and _____ began to crumble.

Finally, on October 19, 1781, General Cornwallis knew he had no other choice but to _____. He was supposed to hand over his sword to General Washington, but he was too embarrassed to face him. Instead, he sent his deputy, claiming he was ill. It was like a bully who talks big but runs away when it's time to face the _____.

The Battle of Yorktown was a turning point in the American Revolution. It was the last major battle, and it effectively sealed America's victory. The brave and clever strategies of the American and _____ forces had paid off, just like when you work hard and smart to win a difficult game.

So, the next time you're playing a strategy game or planning a surprise for your friend, remember the Battle of Yorktown. It's a reminder that with courage, _____ thinking, and the help of good friends, you can overcome even the biggest challenges and make history!

Simplifying Numerical Expressions Involving Integers

Simplifying numerical expressions with integers means making them easier to understand and solve. First, look for any operations inside parentheses and solve those. Next, do any multiplication or division from left to right, and then handle addition or subtraction from left to right. This order helps you know which part to solve first. In the end, you'll have a simpler expression or just one number!

Choose the correct answer for each question below. Need more help? Try Google.

1. What is the result of 8 + (-3)?
a. 11
b. 3
c. 5

2. What is the value of -7 + 2?
a. -5
b. -3
c. -9

3. Simplify: 15 - 4 + (-6)
a. 5
b. 7
c. 11

4. Calculate: -10 + 10 - 5
a. 5
b. 0
c. -5

5. What is the result of 6 * (-2)?
a. 12
b. 8
c. -12

6. What is -3 + (-7)?
a. -12
b. -5
c. -10

7. Simplify: 4 - 9 + 2
a. -3
b. 1
c. -5

8. What is the value of 12 / (-4)?
a. -3
b. 3

9. Calculate: -5 * 3 + 7
a. 2
b. -8
c. 2

10. What is the result of 20 + (-8) + (-4)?
a. 8
b. 12
c. 16

Identify the Adverb(s) Answer Key

1. **Adverb:** beautifully
2. **Adverb:** quickly
3. **Adverb:** always
4. **Adverb:** rarely
5. **Adverb:** loudly
6. **Adverb:** carefully
7. **Adverb:** often
8. **Adverb:** quietly
9. **Adverb:** usually
10. **Adverb:** correctly
11. **Adverb:** never
12. **Adverb:** high
13. **Adverb:** always, twice
14. **Adverb:** slowly
15. **Adverb:** happily

Nucleic Acids

Nucleic acids are special molecules found in all living things that carry genetic information. They include DNA and RNA, which help build and run our bodies by storing and transmitting instructions for making proteins. Think of them as nature's blueprints for life!

Need help? Try Google or your favorite search engine.

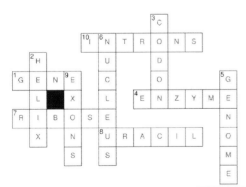

Across
1. A unit of heredity that holds information to build and maintain an organism's cells.
4. A protein that speeds up chemical reactions in the body, including those involving nucleic acids.
7. A sugar molecule that forms part of RNA.
8. A nitrogenous base found in RNA but not in DNA.
10. Non-coding sections of DNA or RNA that are removed before translation into proteins.

Down
2. The shape of DNA, which looks like a twisted ladder.
3. A sequence of three DNA or RNA nucleotides that corresponds to a specific amino acid.
5. The complete set of DNA in an organism, containing all its genes.
6. The cell part where DNA is stored and protected.
9. Sections of DNA or RNA that code for proteins.

EXONS URACIL GENOME
HELIX NUCLEUS RIBOSE
INTRONS GENE ENZYME
CODON

The Haitian Revolution

The Haitian Revolution, which lasted from 1791 to 1804, was a successful slave revolt that took place in the French colony of Saint-Domingue, now known as Haiti. Enslaved Africans, led by figures like Toussaint Louverture, fought against the brutal conditions imposed by French colonial rule. Inspired by the ideals of the French Revolution, they sought freedom and equality. Despite fierce resistance from French forces, the revolutionaries eventually declared independence on January 1, 1804, making Haiti the first nation founded by formerly enslaved people. This revolution not only ended slavery in Haiti but also had a profound impact on abolitionist movements worldwide. It remains a powerful symbol of resistance and the fight for human rights.

	A	B	C	D
1.	Haitian	Haitian	**Haitian**	Haittian
2.	Revolt	Revult	**Revolt**	Revollt
3.	Fredum	Fredom	Freedom	**Freedom**
4.	Equallity	**Equality**	Equaliity	Equaility
5.	Independense	Independanse	Independance	**Independence**
6.	Abolision	Abellision	Abollition	**Abolition**
7.	Collonial	**Colonial**	Colonail	Collonial
8.	Toossaint	Tousaint	**Toussaint**	Toosaint
9.	Loouverture	**Louverture**	Louverture	Looventure
10.	**Resistance**	Resistence	Reesistance	Reasistance
11.	**Enslaved**	Ensclaved	Enslaved	Erislavad
12.	Revolusion	Revollution	Reyollution	**Revolution**
13.	Siant-Domingue	Saintt-Domingue	Siant-Domingue	**Saint-Domingue**
14.	Brutal	Brotal	Brutal	**Brutal**
15.	**Victory**	Victory	Viictory	Vicitory

Science Spelling Words & Their Meanings

Choose the correct answer for each question below. Need more help? Try Google.

1. What is the correct spelling of the term for the study of living organisms?
   a. Bioloyg
   b. Biolgy
   c. [Biology]

2. What is the correct spelling of the term that describes the force that attracts objects toward each other?
   a. Gravety
   b. [Gravity]
   c. Gravty

3. What is the correct spelling of the process by which plants make their food using sunlight?
   a. Photosinthesis
   b. [Photosynthesis]
   c. Photoesynthesis

4. What is the correct spelling of the term for the smallest unit of an element?
   a. Attom
   b. [Atom]
   c. Atem

5. What is the correct spelling of the scientific study of matter and its interactions?
   a. Chemestery
   b. Chemstry
   c. [Chemistry]

6. What is the correct spelling of the term for a substance made up of two or more different elements?
   a. [Compound]
   b. Compond
   c. Compund

7. What is the correct spelling of the process by which water vapor turns into liquid water?
   a. Condensaton
   b. [Condensation]
   c. Condenssation

8. What is the correct spelling of the scientific term for the study of the Earth's physical structure and substance?
   a. Geoligy
   b. Geolgy
   c. [Geology]

9. What is the correct spelling of the term for an organism that produces its own food?
   a. [Autotroph]
   b. Autotroph
   c. Autotrof

10. What is the correct spelling of the term for the natural world, especially as affected by human activity?
    a. Enviroment
    b. [Environment]
    c. Enviorment

Art: Visual

Visual arts are visible art forms such as drawing, painting, sculpture, printmaking, photography, and filmmaking. Design and textile work are also referred to as visual arts. The visual arts have evolved over time. During the __Middle__ Ages, artists became well-known for their paintings, sculptures, and prints. Today, visual arts encompasses a wide range of disciplines.

Drawing is the process of creating a picture with a variety of tools, most commonly __pencils__, crayons, pens, or markers. Artists draw on a variety of surfaces, such as paper or canvas. The first drawings were discovered in caves around 30,000 years ago.

The ancient Egyptians drew on papyrus, while the Greeks and Romans drew on other objects such as __vases__. Drawings were sketches made on parchment in the Middle Ages. Drawing became an art form when paper became widely available during the Renaissance, and it was perfected by Michelangelo, Leonardo Da Vinci, and others.

Painting is frequently referred to as the most important form of visual art. It's all about __splattering__ paint on a canvas or a wall. Painters use a variety of colors and brush strokes to convey their ideas.

Painting is one of the __oldest__ forms of visual art as well. Prehistoric people painted hunting scenes on the walls of old caves. Paintings became popular in ancient Egypt, where __pharaohs'__ tombs were adorned with scenes from everyday Egyptian life.

Printmaking is a type of art that is created by __inking__ a plate and pressing it against the surface of another object. Prints are now mostly made on paper, but they were originally pressed onto cloth or other objects. Plates are frequently made of wood or metal.

Sculptures are __three-dimensional__ works of art created by shaping various materials. Stone, steel, plastic, __ceramics__, and wood are among the most popular. Sculpture is frequently referred to as the plastic arts.

Sculpture can be traced back to ancient __Greece__. Over many centuries, it has played an essential role in various religions around the world. During the Renaissance, Michelangelo was regarded as one of the masters of the art. David, a marble statue of a naked man, was his most famous work.

Music: Musical Terms

Complete the crossword by filling in a word that fits each clue. Fill in the correct answers, one letter per square, both across and down, from the given clues. There will be a gray space between multi-word answers.

Tip: Solve the easy clues first, and then go back and answer the more difficult ones.

Across
2. the highest adult male singing voice; singing falsetto
4. the part of a song that transitions between two main parts
5. a combination of three or more tones sounded simultaneously
8. making up the song or melody as you play
11. a song written for one or more instruments playing solo
12. the highest of the singing voices
13. is a poem set to music with a recurring pattern of both rhyme and meter
14. timing or speed of the music

Down
1. singing without any instruments
3. low, the lowest of the voices and the lowest part of the harmony
6. to play a piece of music sweetly, tender, adoring manner
7. the sound of two or more notes heard simultaneously
9. is a musical interval; the distance between one note
10. played by a single musical instrument or voice
15. a range of voice that is between the bass and the alto
16. the repeating changing of the pitch of a note

CHORD BRIDGE ALTO
HARMONY SOPRANO
IMPROVISATION DOLCE
OCTAVE VIBRATO STANZA
SONATA A CAPPELLA TEMPO
BASS SOLO TENOR

Why It's Important To Apologize: The Power Of Saying Sorry

In this activity, you'll see lots of grammatical *errors*. Correct all the grammar mistakes you see.

There are **9** mistakes in this passage. 0 capitals missing. 2 unnecessary capitals. 2 repeated words. 1 incorrect homophone. 4 incorrectly spelled words.

While it might be difficult to apologize, doing so is a crucial step in mending broken bonds and fostering new connections with others. A genuine apology shows concern for the person we have wronged while also accepting responsibility for our actions.

Sincere apologies demonstrate how much we care about ~~the tho~~ the other person by demonstrating that we are willing to ~~take take~~ take responsibility for our actions and work toward repairing the damage we may ~~hive~~ have caused. By doing ~~So,~~ so, we can begin to restore our mutual trust and create more respectful relationships ~~wath~~ with ~~won~~ one another.

On the other hand, if you ~~dun't~~ don't apologize when you ~~shoold,~~ should, you could end up doing more harm than good and damaging relationships ~~Te~~ to the point where trust is impossible to regain for years.

As a result, it's important to learn how and when to apologize so that you may improve your communication and strengthen your bonds with others in your personal and professional lives.

Order of Operations Pretest

When it comes to math you should always do your problems in the right order. If you don't work your problems in the correct order you may end up with the wrong answer. Basically, the order of operations means the correct order in math.

1. Do everything _____ of brackets first.
   a. it doesn't matter which one you do first
   b. outside
   c. inside

2. When working with multiplication and division, you should perform them_____.
   a. right to left
   b. right or left
   c. left to right

3. For the problem 30 + 1 - 2 x 7 + 6 ÷ (5 x 2), what portion of the problem would you do first?
   a. Do the addition.
   b. Do the multiplication.
   c. Do the brackets.

4. For the problem 5 x 10 - (12 x 8 - 10) + 3 x 10 ÷ 5, how do you work the brackets?
   a. It don't matter which one I do first.
   b. Do the subtraction in the brackets first.
   c. Do the multiplication in the brackets first.

5. When working with addition and subtraction, you should perform them_____.
   a. neither left or right
   b. right to left
   c. left to right

6. If you have a bunch of operations of the same rank, you would operate from_____.
   a. left to right
   b. right to left
   c. both a and b

7. First, I do all operations that lie inside parentheses or brackets, then I_____.
   a. do any work with addition and subtraction
   b. do any work with exponents or radicals
   c. do any work from right to left

Comparative Adjectives

Comparative adjectives help us compare two things to show which has more or less of a certain quality. We usually add "-er" to the end of an adjective to make it comparative, like "taller" or "smaller." If the adjective is long, like "beautiful," we use "more" before it instead, like "more beautiful." We use the word "than" to show what we are comparing, like "Sarah is taller than John." This way, we can talk about the differences between things easily!

Choose the correct answer for each question below. Need more help? Try Google.

1. What is the comparative form of 'big'?
   a. more big
   b. bigger
   c. biggest

2. Which of the following is the correct comparative form of 'good'?
   a. gooder
   b. more good
   c. better

3. How do you form the comparative of 'happy'?
   a. more happy
   b. happier
   c. happyer

4. What is the comparative form of 'bad'?
   a. badder
   b. more bad
   c. worse

5. Which comparative form is correct for 'fast'?
   a. faster
   b. fastest
   c. more fast

6. What is the comparative of 'funny'?
   a. more funny
   b. funnier
   c. funniest

7. What is the correct comparative form of 'tall'?
   a. tallest
   b. more tall
   c. taller

8. Which of these is the comparative form of 'easy'?
   a. more easy
   b. easiest
   c. easier

9. What is the comparative form for 'old'?
   a. oldest
   b. more old
   c. older

10. What is the correct comparative form of 'rich'?
    a. more rich
    b. richer
    c. richest

Exoplanets

Exoplanets are planets that orbit stars outside our solar system. They come in various sizes and types, some similar to Earth and others vastly different. Scientists discover exoplanets using telescopes and special techniques like the transit method, where they observe a star's light dimming as a planet passes in front of it. Studying exoplanets helps us understand more about how planets form and whether life might exist elsewhere in the universe. Many exoplanets are found within a "habitable zone," where conditions could support liquid water. Learning about exoplanets expands our knowledge of the vast and diverse cosmos.

Directions: Carefully circle the correct spelling combinations of words.

	A	B	C	D
1.	Exoplanet	**Exoplanet**	Exuplanet	Exuplanet
2.	Orbyt	Orrbit	Orrbyt	**Orbit**
3.	**Telescope**	Telescope	Teliescope	Teliescope
4.	Trransit	**Transit**	Transyt	Trransyt
5.	Attmousphere	Atmousphere	**Atmosphere**	Attmosphere
6.	Habitible	Habittible	Habitable	**Habitable**
7.	Dettecion	Dettecion	**Detection**	Detecsion
8.	Light-yaer	**Light-year**	Light-yaer	Light-year
9.	Disssovery	Disscovery	Disssovery	**Discovery**
10.	Spectrouscopy	Spectrouscopy	**Spectroscopy**	Spectrouscopy
11.	Asstronomy	**Astronomy**	Asctronomy	Astrunomy
12.	Pllanetary	Pllanetari	Planetari	**Planetary**
13.	Universe	Univerce	**Universe**	Univerce
14.	Celestail	Cellestail	Cellestal	**Celestial**
15.	Extraterrestrail	Extraterestrail	**Extraterrestrial**	Extraterrestrial

---

Henry Ford

During this exercise, fill in the blanks with the correct word. Need help? Try Google or your favorite search engine.

Innovation	Model	Innovation	machines	vehicle
Pioneer	car	Michigan	Industrialist	Entrepreneur
quantities	manufacturing	Engineer	Efficiency	resources

1. Automobile - A _vehicle_ with an engine used for transporting people, like a car.
2. Assembly Line - A _manufacturing_ method where a product is put together in steps by different workers.
3. Ford Motor Company - The _car_ company founded by Henry Ford in 1903.
4. _Model_ T - The first affordable car made by Henry Ford, introduced in 1908.
5. _Innovation_ - The act of creating new ideas or methods.
6. Detroit - The city in _Michigan_ where Henry Ford started his car company.
7. _Engineer_ - A person who designs and builds complex products, like cars.
8. Efficiency - Doing something in the best way with the least waste of time and _resources_.
9. Mass Production - Making large _quantities_ of a product quickly and cheaply.
10. _Industrialist_ - A person involved in the ownership and management of industries.
11. Mechanic - A person skilled in repairing and maintaining _machines_, especially cars.
12. _Pioneer_ - Someone who is among the first to explore or settle a new area or develop a new idea.
13. _Entrepreneur_ - A person who starts and runs a business, taking on financial risks.
14. _Innovation_ - The introduction of new ideas, goods, services, and practices.
15. _Efficiency_ - Achieving maximum productivity with minimum wasted effort or expense.

Today is Alphabetical Word Order Day!

Alphabetical order is a way to keep information in order. It makes it easier to find what you need. Additionally, organizing your spelling words alphabetically will assist you in remembering your word list.

To arrange words alphabetically, starting with the first letter of each word. If a word begins with the same letter as another, you should evaluate the second letter. In some instances, if two or more words share the same first and second letters, you may need to consider the third letter.

Carefully put the words in alphabetical order.

Word Bank	Answers
executive	1. achievement
analysis	2. acres
reprimand	3. analysis
hygiene	4. atmosphere
ordinarily	5. candidate
informant	6. executive
atmosphere	7. humid
mysterious	8. hygiene
receipt	9. informant
morale	10. kettle
candidate	11. management
humid	12. morale
management	13. mysterious
achievement	14. ordinarily
politely	15. politely
kettle	16. receipt
acres	17. reprimand

Art: Pablo Picasso

His father was a _painter_ who also taught art. Pablo has always enjoyed drawing since he was a child.

According to legend, his first word was "piz," which is _Spanish_ for "pencil."

Pablo enrolled in a _prestigious_ art school in _Barcelona_ when he was fourteen years old. He transferred to another school in _Madrid_ a few years later.

Pablo's close friend _Carlos_ _Casagemas_ committed _suicide_ in 1901. Pablo became _depressed_.

He began painting in Paris around the same time. For the next four years, the color _blue_ dominated his paintings.

He depicted people with elongated _features_ and faces in his paintings.

Pablo eventually _recovered_ from his depression. He also had feelings for a _French_ model.

The Rose Period is a term used by art _historians_ to describe this period in Pablo's life.

He also started painting happier scenes like _circuses_.

Picasso began experimenting with a new _painting_ style in 1907. He _collaborated_ with another artist, Georges Braque.

The sections are then reassembled and painted from various perspectives and _angles_.

He would use _sand_ or plaster in his paint to give it texture in this area.

He would also add dimension to his paintings by using materials such as colored paper, _newspapers_, and wallpaper.

Although Picasso continued to experiment with Cubism, he went through a period of painting more _classical-style_ paintings around 1921.

They frequently resemble something out of a nightmare or a _dream_.

Guernica and The Red Armchair are two examples of surrealism's _influence_ on Picasso's art.

Many consider him to be one of the _greatest_ artists in all of history.

He painted several self-portraits near the end of his _life_.

He _died_ a year later, on April 8, 1973, at the age of 91.

Music: String Family Instruments

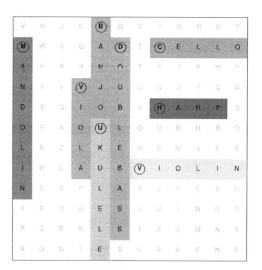

Violin → Viola ↓ Cello → Double Bass ↓ Harp → Banjo ↓ Mandolin ↓ Ukulele ↓

8 words in Wordsearch. 5 vertical, 3 horizontal, 0 diagonal. (0 reversed.)

Paranoia

In this activity, you'll see lots of grammatical *errors*. Correct all the grammar mistakes you see.

> There are **9 mistakes** in this passage. 1 capital missing. 2 unnecessary capitals. 1 repeated word. 1 incorrect homophone. 4 incorrectly spelled words.

Paranoia behavior is a psychological condition where someone feels ~~haghly~~ highly suspicious and fearful of the world around ~~tham~~ them. It differs ~~from from~~ from healthy caution and can impede normal functioning, making it difficult for those with paranoia to participate in meaningful relationships or just get through a typical day. ~~the~~ The most important thing to remember about ~~paranied~~ paranoid behavior is that it can also be a symptom of larger mental health issues and should be discussed with a professional to ensure proper support is in place.

Thoughts of suspicion are not always the result of paranoia. There are times when we should all be wary and suspicious. It's perfectly ~~Reasonable~~ reasonable ~~too~~ to suspect something, provided you have good reason to do so. If, for instance, a large number of people on your street have been victimized, it is reasonable to be cautious about ~~Your~~ your ~~persunal~~ personal safety when strolling around. An accurate suspicion of danger can save your life.

One-Tenth or One-Hundredth More or Less

One-tenth means dividing something into 10 equal parts, and one-hundredth means dividing it into 100 equal parts. If you have one-tenth more, you're adding a small piece (1 out of 10) to your total. If it's one-tenth less, you're taking away that same small piece. One-hundredth more or less works the same way, but the pieces are even smaller, since 100 parts are smaller than 10 parts. So, you're adjusting the amount by tiny bits!

Choose the correct answer for each question below. Need help? Try Google.

1. What is one-tenth of 100?
   a. 5
   b. 20
   c. **10**

2. If you have 50 and you take away one-tenth, how much do you have left?
   a. 55
   b. **45**
   c. 40

3. What is one-hundredth of 2500?
   a. 2.5
   b. **25**
   c. 250

4. If a product costs $200 and is marked down by one-hundredth, what is the new price?
   a. $198
   b. **$199**
   c. $201

5. What is one-tenth more than 30?
   a. 29
   b. 31
   c. **33**

6. If you have 80 and you add one-tenth of it, what is the total?
   a. 70
   b. 90
   c. **88**

7. What is one-hundredth less than 1?
   a. 0.90
   b. 1.01
   c. **0.99**

8. How much is one-tenth of 450?
   a. 40
   b. 50
   c. **45**

9. If a value is decreased by one-hundredth, what is the new value of 500?
   a. **499.99**
   b. 505
   c. 500.01

10. What is one-tenth of 900?
   a. **90**
   b. 100
   c. 80

Learning Comma Usage Answer Key:

1. Incorrect (Add commas after "pencils" and "erasers"): I want to buy pencils, erasers, and notebooks.

2. Incorrect (Add commas after "Monday" and "June 5"): We went to the beach on Monday, June 5, 2023.

3. Incorrect (Add commas after "New York" and "New York"): My friend Mary lives in New York, New York.

4. Correct

5. Correct

6. Incorrect (Add commas after "milk" and "eggs"): We need to buy milk, eggs, and bread from the store.

7. Correct

8. Correct

9. Incorrect (Add commas after "Los Angeles," "California," and "United States"): The dog named Spot lives in Los Angeles, California, United States.

10. Correct

11. Incorrect (Add commas after "Tuesday" and "May 10"): I was born on Tuesday, May 10, 2010.

12. Incorrect (Add comma before "Anna")

13. Incorrect (Add commas after "London" and "England"): Our school is located in London, England, United Kingdom.

14. Correct

15. Correct

Rock Cycle

ANSWER SHEET

First, read all the way through. After that, go back and fill in the blanks. You can skip the blanks you're unsure about and finish them later.

| tectonic | transformed | lava | particles | chemically |
| erosion | metamorphic | time | layers | shale |

The rock cycle is a continuous process that describes how rocks are formed, broken down, and transformed over time. This cycle helps explain the dynamic nature of Earth's crust and the different types of rocks we find.

There are three main types of rocks: igneous, sedimentary, and metamorphic . Each type forms through different processes and can be transformed into another type over time .

Igneous rocks form from the cooling and solidification of molten rock, called magma or lava . When magma cools slowly beneath the Earth's surface, it forms intrusive igneous rocks like granite. If lava cools quickly on the surface, it creates extrusive igneous rocks like basalt.

Sedimentary rocks are formed from the accumulation of small particles , like sand, silt, and clay, which are carried by wind, water, or ice and deposited in layers . Over time, these layers become compacted and cemented together, forming rocks like sandstone, shale, and limestone. Sedimentary rocks often contain fossils, which provide clues about Earth's past life and environments.

Metamorphic rocks are created when existing rocks are subjected to heat and pressure, causing them to change physically and chemically without melting. This transformation can occur deep within the Earth or at tectonic plate boundaries. Examples of metamorphic rocks include marble, which forms from limestone, and schist, which forms from shale .

The rock cycle is driven by Earth's internal heat, gravitational forces, and external processes like weathering and erosion . For example, igneous rocks can be broken down into sediments by weathering and erosion, eventually forming sedimentary rocks. These sedimentary rocks can be buried and subjected to heat and pressure, transforming into metamorphic rocks. If the conditions are right, metamorphic rocks can melt and become magma, starting the cycle anew.

The Mayflower Compact

ANSWER SHEET

The Mayflower Compact was a written agreement created by the Pilgrims in 1620. It was signed aboard the Mayflower, their ship, before they landed at Plymouth in present-day Massachusetts. The document established a basic form of government and laws for the new colony. It emphasized the importance of working together for the common good. The Mayflower Compact is significant because it was one of the first steps toward self-government in America. It set a precedent for future democratic practices in the colonies.

	A	B	C	D
1.	Mayflower	Mayflower	**Mayflower**	Mayflower
2.	Cumpact	Compact	**Compact**	Cumpact
3.	Pilgrims	**Pilgrims**	Pylgrims	Pylgrims
4.	Plymooth	Plymooth	Plymouth	**Plymouth**
5.	**Agreement**	Agrement	Agreient	Agreement
6.	Cullony	Cullony	**Colony**	Collony
7.	Shipboard	**Shipboard**	Shipboard	Shipbuard
8.	Governmment	**Government**	Goverment	Goverment
9.	Lawsc	Laws	**Laws**	Lawss
10.	**Precedent**	Presedent	Preoedent	Prreedent
11.	Demoracy	Democracy	Demucracy	**Democracy**
12.	**Settlement**	Setiement	Settlenment	Settlenment
13.	Signers	**Signers**	Sygners	Sygners
14.	Leaderrship	**Leadership**	Laedership	Laedership
15.	Ameryca	Ameryca	**America**	America

Today Is Spelling Day! Spelling Words Sort

Alphabetical order is a way to keep information in order. It makes it easier to find what you need. Additionally, organizing your spelling words alphabetically will assist you in remembering your word list.

To arrange words alphabetically, starting with the first letter of each word. If a word begins with the same letter as another, you should evaluate the second letter. In some instances, if two or more words share the same first and second letters, you may need to consider the third letter.

Carefully put these words in alphabetical order.

cinnamon	1. athlete
idol	2. baggage
elementary	3. boundary
category	4. capital
concentrate	5. category
inherit	6. cinnamon
committed	7. committed
capital	8. concentrate
fabricate	9. elementary
heroic	10. fabricate
boundary	11. heroic
innocent	12. idol
irate	13. inherit
baggage	14. innocent
athlete	15. irate

Art: Roman Portrait Sculptures

Alexander	aristocrats	ancestral	shrine	rewarded
sculpture	pattern	mosaics	marble	artistic

Portrait _sculpture_ has been practiced since the beginning of Roman history. It was most likely influenced by the Roman practice of creating _ancestral_ images. When a Roman man died, his family made a wax sculpture of his face and kept it in a special _shrine_ at home. Because these sculptures were more like records of a person's life than works of art, the emphasis was on realistic detail rather than _artistic_ beauty.

As Rome became more prosperous and gained access to Greek sculptors, Roman _aristocrats_ known as patricians began creating these portraits from stone rather than wax.

Roman sculpture was about more than just honoring the dead; it was also about honoring the living. Important Romans were _rewarded_ for their valor or greatness by having statues of themselves erected and displayed in public. This is one of the earliest of these types of statues that we've discovered, and the _pattern_ continued all the way until the Republic's demise.

The mosaic is the only form of Roman art that has yet to be discussed. The Romans adored mosaics and created them with exquisite skill. The Romans created _mosaics_ of unprecedented quality and detail using cubes of naturally colored _marble_. The floor mosaic depicting _Alexander_ the Great at the Battle of Issus is probably the most famous Roman mosaic.

Sound Waves Crossword

Sound waves are a form of mechanical wave, meaning they require a medium to travel through. The speed of sound is affected by the properties of the medium it is traveling through, such as temperature, pressure, and density.

Match the clues to the words. Need help? Try Google.

Across

1. A rapid movement or shaking of the air that produces sound or a sensation of movement.
2. The thin membranes in the inner ear that vibrate in response to sound waves and help the brain interpret them as sounds.
4. A period of 100 years.
7. The way a person behaves or acts in response to a particular situation or event.
9. To transmit information, such as audio or video, over radio waves so it can be received by multiple people simultaneously.

Down

3. Someone who is devoted to studying, researching, and understanding the fundamental nature of knowledge, reality, and existence.
5. The act of discovering something that was previously unknown.
6. People engaged in research and experimentation with the aim of gaining new knowledge about different topics.
8. Small electronic devices designed to make life easier or more enjoyable.
9. Pleasingly attractive, especially in appearance; having qualities that delight the senses and stir emotion.

> PHILOSOPHER BEAUTIFUL
> BROADCAST EARDRUMS
> GADGETS VIBRATION
> CENTURY DISCOVERY
> SCIENTISTS BEHAVIOR

Reproductive Health Words You Should Know

Match the clues to the words. Need help? Try Google.

Across

3. The process of childbirth.
5. The first time a person gets their period.
7. A breast/chest cancer screening that takes x-rays of the breast/chest tissue to find lumps.
8. The tightening and releasing of the muscles that stop urination in order to prevent and improve urinary incontinence.
5. The inability to become pregnant or to cause a pregnancy.

Down

2. A treatment that prevents cervical cancer.
4. The lips of the vulva.
5. A health care provider who is trained to assist in childbirth.
6. Menstrual bleeding that's heavier or longer lasting than usual.
9. Being unable to control urination or bowel movements.

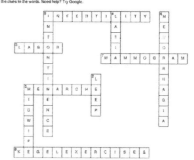

Conversions

Sentence Building: Unscramble the sentences!

(Use a separate sheet of paper to write out sentences if needed.)

1. Conversions involve changing one unit of measurement to another, like inches to centimeters.

   centimeters · another · to · changing · inches · measurement · Conversions · involve · to · one · of · unit · like

2. To convert from miles to kilometers, you multiply the number of miles by 1.60934

   in · To · you · kilometers, · multiply · by · convert · from · miles · the · miles · 1.60934 · of · number

3. Understanding conversions is important in science, math, and everyday life.

   and · conversions · everyday · in · Understanding · life. · important · math. · science. · is

4. In cooking, you might need to convert tablespoons to teaspoons.

   to · In · tablespoons · need · cooking, · convert · you · teaspoons · might · to

5. Temperature conversions can be tricky; for example, converting Fahrenheit to Celsius requires a formula.

   to · Fahrenheit · tricky; · a · can · converting · for · Celsius · Temperature · conversions · requires · example. · formula · be

6. When converting from pounds to kilograms, you divide the number of pounds by 2.20462

   pounds · When · to · the · 2.20462 · by · converting · you · from · of · pounds · divide · kilograms, · number

7. Metric units, like meters and liters, are often easier to convert because they use a base-10 system.

   easier · because · liters, · they · are · often · to · Metric · units, · use · system, · a · like · meters · base-10 · and · convert

8. Currency conversions help people understand the value of money when traveling to different countries.

   to · when · Currency · of · conversions · different · countries. · people · money · the · traveling · value · help · understand

9. Converting fractions to decimals is a common type of conversion in mathematics.

   conversion · Converting · of · type · mathematics. · decimals · common · a · fractions · to · in · is

10. Engineers and architects regularly perform conversions to ensure their measurements are accurate.

    and · their · are · regularly · ensure · perform · measurements · accurate · conversions · Engineers · to · architects

---

Types of Context Clues Answer Key

Multiple Choice Questions

1. B. Stubborn

2. D. Non-professional

3. D. Secrecy

4. B. Exhausted

True or False

5. True

6. False (Aroma refers to a pleasant smell)

7. False (Punctuality means being on time, but the sentence suggests the opposite)

8. False (Fragile means easily broken or delicate)

Short Answer

9. Innovative means introducing new ideas; original and creative in thinking.

10. Monotonous means dull, tedious, and repetitious; lacking in variety and interest.

11. Culinary relates to cooking or the kitchen.

12. Copious means abundant in supply or quantity.

Soil Composition

Soil composition refers to what makes up soil, which is essential for plant growth. Soil is a mixture of minerals, organic matter, water, and air. The minerals come from broken-down rocks, while organic matter includes decomposed plants and animals. Water and air in the soil help roots get the nutrients they need. Different types of soil, like sandy, clay, or loamy, have different compositions. Understanding soil composition helps us grow healthy plants and manage farmland effectively.

Directions: Carefully circle the correct spelling combinations of words.

	A	B	C	D
1.	Mynerals	**Minerals**	Minerrals	Mynerrals
2.	Organyc	Orrganyc	Organic	**Organic**
3.	Humus	**Humus**	Humuss	Humusc
4.	Sandstune	**Sandstone**	Sandsctone	Sandstone
5.	Loamy	**Loamy**	Lotmy	Laumy
6.	Textdure	Textore	**Texture**	Texttore
7.	Porosity	**Porosity**	Porrousity	Porousity
8.	**Microbes**	Micrubes	Micrrubes	Microbes
9.	Aerasion	Aerration	Aerasion	**Aeration**
10.	**Nutrients**	Nutreints	Nutreints	Nutrients
11.	Erotion	**Erosion**	Errobion	Errosion
12.	**Decompose**	Decomposse	Decompouse	Decompousse
13.	Ferrtiliti	Ferrtility	**Fertility**	Fertilli
14.	**Sediment**	Sedinment	Sedimentt	Sedimentt
15.	Compaotsion	Compacttion	Compaosion	**Compaction**

Cowboys and Outlaws

During this exercise, fill in the blanks with the correct word. Need help? Try Google or your favorite search engine.

criminal's	outlaw	Sheriff	Posse	animals
rope	Revolver	farm	Frontier	cows
wagon	law	Saloon	Duel	Cowboy

1. _Cowboy_ : A person who herds and tends cattle on a ranch, often on horseback.

2. Cattle: Large farm animals, like _cows_, that are raised for their meat or milk.

3. Ranch: A large _farm_ where cattle and other animals are raised.

4. Lasso: A long _rope_ with a loop used by cowboys to catch animals.

5. Outlaw: A person who breaks the _law_ and lives outside of legal authority.

6. _Sheriff_ : An officer who keeps law and order in a town or county.

7. _Saloon_ : A place where people in the Old West went to drink, eat, and socialize.

8. Bandit: Another word for an _outlaw_ who robs people.

9. _Posse_ : A group of people, usually led by a sheriff, who chase and capture criminals.

10. Wanted Poster: A sign showing a _criminal's_ picture and offering a reward for their capture.

11. _Duel_ : A fight between two people, often using guns, to settle a dispute.

12. _Revolver_ : A type of handgun commonly used by cowboys and outlaws.

13. Herd: A group of _animals_, like cattle, that live and move together.

14. _Frontier_ : The edge of settled land where pioneers lived and new areas were explored.

15. Stagecoach: A horse-drawn _wagon_ used for carrying passengers and mail across the country.

Vocabulary: Community Services

Directions: Read the words. Sort the words into the community services in which they belong.

insurance	sick	injured	emergency	firefighter	doctor
driver's license	video	adult education	nurse	ticket	EMS worker
Principal	students	teacher	magazines	officer	return
loan	learning	junior high	borrow	newspapers	librarian
medicine	books	pharmacist	911	high school	pharmacy
elementary school					

Hospital (8)	Library (8)	Police/Fire Department (7)	School (8)
doctor	librarian	officer	teacher
nurse	books	firefighter	Principal
pharmacy	video	EMS worker	students
pharmacist	magazines	911	elementary school
sick	newspapers	ticket	junior high
injured	borrow	emergency	high school
medicine	loan	driver's license	adult education
insurance	return		learning

Art: Leonardo da Vinci

1. Where was he born?
a. America
b. England
c. Italy

2. What was his first name?
a. Leonardo
b. Emilio
c. Davinci

3. As a child, he wanted to____?
a. swim in the lake
b. fly in the sky
c. climb a mountain

4. He drew pictures of
a. buildings
b. food
c. nature

5. How did he get better at drawing?
a. He watched YouTube.
b. He had a friend who helped.
c. He studied.

6. His most famous painting is____?
a. Mona Dona
b. Lisa Mona
c. Mona Lisa

7. Leonardo was _____ handed.
a. left
b. used both hands
c. right

8. The Mona Lisa is a portrait of the wife of a _____ official.
a. United States
b. Florentine
c. Army

9. Who Stole the Mona Lisa?
a. Vincenzo Peruggia
b. Veronica Parkay
c. Vincent Paisley

10. Can you buy the real Mona Lisa?
a. The painting cannot be bought or sold according to French heritage law
b. The painting is currently on sale for 1 million dollars.
c. The painting can be bought at your local art gallery

MUSIC: The Orchestra Vocab Words

Unscramble the names of the instruments found in the orchestra.

violin	strings	double bass	harp	cello	clarinet
timpani	oboe	trumpet	piano	french horn	flute
bassoon	saxaphone	cymbals	xylophone	trombone	drums
woodwind	percussion	brass	conductor		

1. lueft — f l u t e
2. iinvol — v i o l i n
3. obeo — o b o e
4. nfrech honr — f r e n c h h o r n
5. nabooss — b a s s o o n
6. rlniatce — c l a r i n e t
7. sdrum — d r u m s
8. nipmiat — t i m p a n i
9. nsrtgis — s t r i n g s
10. odonidww — w o o d w i n d
11. asrbs — b r a s s

12. rucspiosne — p e r c u s s i o n
13. eclol — c e l l o
14. aprh — h a r p
15. edolub bssa — d o u b l e b a s s
16. eupmttr — t r u m p e t
17. elbmoron — t r o m b o n e
18. phexloyno — x y l o p h o n e
19. lscmbay — c y m b a l s
20. odornuctc — c o n d u c t o r
21. noapi — p i a n o
22. phxasoaen — s a x a p h o n e

Heart Crossword

Match the clues to the words. Need help? Try Google.

```
5F                    1D
 A        7H   9P A I N    3A
4T I S S U E        A      B
 L        A         G      N
 U        2P R E V E N T I O N
 R        T         O      R
 E      6C H E S T         M
        I                  A
8V E S S E L
```

Across
2. the act of hindering
4. part of an organism consisting of an aggregate of cells
6. the part of the human torso between the neck and the diaphragm
8. an object used as a container, especially for liquids
9. a physical feeling of suffering or discomfort

Down
1. identifying the nature or cause of some phenomenon
3. not typical or usual or regular
5. an act that does not succeed
7. the hollow muscular organ located behind the sternum

PREVENTION HEART
CHEST FAILURE
VESSEL PAIN
ABNORMAL DIAGNOSIS
TISSUE

Time Zones

Time zones are like different parts of the world having their own clocks. Because the Earth is so big, the sun rises and sets at different times in different places. So, people in one place might be eating breakfast while others are already having dinner! Time zones help everyone know what time it is in different places. If you travel far, like from New York to London, you might have to change your clock to match the new time zone.

Choose the correct answer for each question below. Need help? Try Google.

1. What is the time zone for New York City?
   a. Pacific Standard Time (PST)
   b. Eastern Standard Time (EST)
   c. Central Standard Time (CST)

2. Which time zone is 10 hours ahead of UTC?
   a. UTC+5
   b. UTC+10
   c. UTC+6

3. What time zone does London operate on during Daylight Saving Time?
   a. Central European Time (CET)
   b. British Summer Time (BST)
   c. Greenwich Mean Time (GMT)

4. Which city is in the Central Time Zone?
   a. Chicago
   b. Los Angeles
   c. New York

5. When does Daylight Saving Time typically end in the United States?
   a. Last Sunday in March
   b. First Sunday in November
   c. Last Sunday in October

6. What is the time difference between UTC and Indian Standard Time?
   a. UTC+5
   b. UTC+5:30
   c. UTC+6

7. Which of the following regions does NOT observe Daylight Saving Time?
   a. Hawaii
   b. California
   c. Florida

8. What is the time zone abbreviation for Japan?
   a. CST (China Standard Time)
   b. JST (Japan Standard Time)
   c. JDT (Japan Daylight Time)

9. Which time zone is used in the majority of western Canada?
   a. Pacific Standard Time (PST)
   b. Mountain Standard Time (MST)
   c. Central Standard Time (CST)

10. What time zone is used in Brazil's capital, Brasilia?
    a. Brasilia Time (BRT)
    b. Amazon Time (AMT)
    c. Acre Time (ACT)

Identify The Various Parts of Grammar

Across

1. the first word in a noun group
2. a word used to describe a noun
3. the first part of a sentence is called the ....
7. this tells us how many of a noun (some / ten / a few)
10. a sentence that uses a conjunction to join two independent clauses
11. a sentence with a dependent clause and one or more independent clauses
12. one conjunction is ....
15. a clause beginning with if / when / because is called ....
18. the last part of a sentence is called ....
19. a phrase beginning with a preposition is called ....

Down

3. What type of sentence is one independent clause
4. an independent clause can only have one ....
5. the last word of a noun group
6. a / on / the are called ....
8. this / that / these / those are called ....
9. tells us who owns the noun
13. we change the verb to make past ... ...
14. a story written or spoken in past tense
16. a clause that contains the full meaning is called ....
20. the conjunctions so and because give us a result and ....

ADJECTIVE INDEPENDENT
COMPLEX TENSE DEPENDENT
BECAUSE VERB
POSSESSIVE QUANTIFIER
COMPOUND SIMPLE
PREPOSITIONAL RECOUNT
DETERMINER ARTICLE
OBJECT REASON SUBJECT
DEMONSTRATIVE NOUN

Constellations

First, read all the way through. After that, go back and fill in the blanks. You can skip the blanks you're unsure about and finish them later.

Major	seasons	navigation	Polaris	sky
Stargazing	orbits	astronomers	north	stars

Constellations are patterns of _stars_ in the night sky that people have imagined to look like pictures or shapes. These star patterns have been used for thousands of years to tell stories, navigate, and keep track of time.

There are 88 official constellations recognized by _astronomers_ today. Each constellation has its own unique shape and story. For example, one of the most famous constellations is the Big Dipper, which looks like a large spoon or dipper. The Big Dipper is part of a larger constellation called Ursa _Major_, or the Great Bear.

Another well-known constellation is Orion, the Hunter. Orion is easy to spot because of the three bright stars that form his "belt." You can also see his "shoulders" and "legs" made up of other bright stars. According to Greek mythology, Orion was a great hunter who was placed in the _sky_ by the gods.

Constellations are important for _navigation_. Before modern technology, sailors and travelers used the stars to find their way. One very helpful constellation for navigation is the Little Dipper, which includes the North Star, or _Polaris_. Polaris always points _north_ and helps people figure out which direction they are facing.

Constellations also help us keep track of time and _seasons_. As Earth _orbits_ the Sun, different constellations become visible at different times of the year. For instance, in the winter, you might see Orion in the sky, while in the summer, you might see Scorpius, the Scorpion.

Stargazing is a fun activity that can help you learn more about constellations. All you need is a clear night sky and a little bit of patience. You can even use a star map or a stargazing app to help you find and identify different constellations.

So next time you look up at the night sky, try to spot some constellations and imagine the stories behind them. It's like having a giant, sparkling picture book right above your head!

The Red Scare

During this exercise, fill in the blanks with the correct word. Need help? Try Google or your favorite search engine.

communism	atomic	Patriotism	Espionage	Loyalty
Fearmongering	Propaganda	Atomic	Subversion	Soviet
Iron	Cold	political	McCarthyism	Act

1. Red Scare - A period of intense fear of **communism** in the United States.
2. Communism - A **political** system where all property is publicly owned, and each person works and is paid according to their abilities and needs.
3. **Cold** War - The rivalry between the United States and the Soviet Union after World War II, which heightened fears of communism.
4. **McCarthyism** - The practice of making accusations of subversion or treason without proper evidence, named after Senator Joseph McCarthy.
5. **Atomic** Spies - Individuals accused of spying for the Soviet Union and passing information about the atomic bomb.
6. Smith **Act** - A law that made it illegal to advocate for the violent overthrow of the government, used to target communists.
7. **Soviet** Union - The communist nation that was a major adversary of the United States during the Cold War.
8. **Espionage** - The act of spying, especially by government agents.
9. **Subversion** - The act of trying to undermine the authority or integrity of an established system or institution.
10. **Patriotism** - Devotion to one's country; during the Red Scare, questioning someone's patriotism was common if they were suspected of communist sympathies.
11. Cold War **Propaganda** - Information, especially biased or misleading, used to promote anti-communist sentiments.
12. **Loyalty** Oaths - Pledges of allegiance to the United States, required of many government employees to prove they were not communists.
13. Rosenberg Trial - The trial of Julius and Ethel Rosenberg, who were executed for allegedly passing **atomic** secrets to the Soviet Union.
14. **Iron** Curtain - The metaphorical division between the communist nations of Eastern Europe and the democratic nations of Western Europe.
15. **Fearmongering** - Spreading fear to influence public opinion, often used during the Red Scare to control attitudes toward communism.

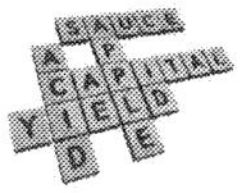

Vocab Crossword Puzzle

ANSWER SHEET

Solve the puzzle below with the correct vocabulary word.

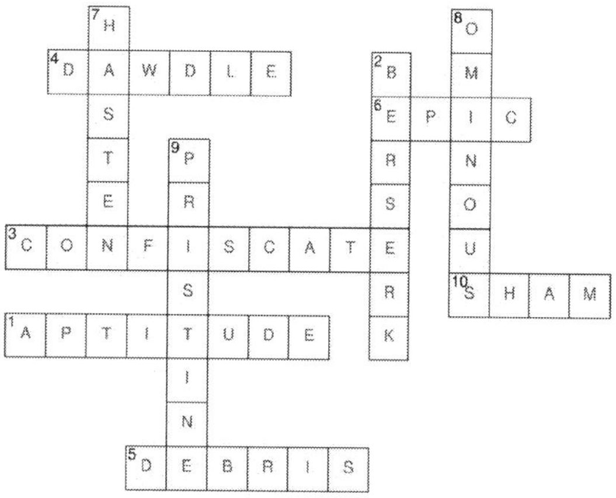

Crossword grid answers:
- 7 Down: HASTER / 4 Across: DAWDLE / 8 Down: OMINOUS
- 6 Across: EPIC
- 9 Down: PRISTINE
- 3 Across: CONFISCATE
- 10 Across: SHAM
- 1 Across: APTITUDE
- 5 Across: DEBRIS
- 2 Down: BERSERK

Across
1. capability; ability; innate or acquired capacity for something;
3. to seize by or as if by authority; appropriate summarily;
4. to waste time; idle; trifle; loiter; to move slowly
5. the remains of anything broken down or destroyed; ruins; rubble;
6. heroic; majestic; impressively great;
10. something that is not what it purports to be; a spurious imitation; fraud or hoax.

Down
2. violently or destructively frenzied; wild; crazed; deranged;
7. to move or act with haste; proceed with haste; hurry;
8. portending evil or harm; foreboding; threatening; inauspicious;
9. having its original purity; uncorrupted or unsullied.

OMINOUS DEBRIS
APTITUDE BERSERK
SHAM HASTEN PRISTINE
CONFISCATE DAWDLE
EPIC

Health Cause & Effect

ANSWER SHEET

Staying healthy means taking care of your body so you can grow strong and feel good. Eating lots of fruits and vegetables is a great start because they're full of vitamins that help your body fight off sickness. It's also important to drink plenty of water every day to keep hydrated. Try to choose snacks like nuts or yogurt instead of too much candy or chips, which can make you feel sluggish.

Being active is another key part of staying healthy. Activities like running, jumping rope, or playing sports with friends are not only fun but also keep your heart and muscles strong. Even walking your dog or dancing in your room counts as being active!

Getting enough sleep each night is crucial too because it helps your body and brain rest and recharge. Try to stick to a regular bedtime and limit screen time before bed to help you fall asleep easier.

Lastly, always remember to wash your hands regularly to keep germs away, especially before eating. Making these healthy choices every day will help you feel your best and do well in school and play!

#				
1	D	Smoking	→	Lung cancer
2	B	Deforestation	→	Loss of biodiversity
3	C	High sugar intake	→	Diabetes
4	I	Excessive alcohol consumption	→	Liver disease
5	G	Air pollution	→	Respiratory diseases
6	H	Sedentary lifestyle	→	Obesity
7	A	Climate change	→	Extreme weather events
8	E	Poor diet	→	Heart disease
9	F	Stress	→	Mental health issues
10	J	Neglect	→	Child development problems

Find the Change, Price, or Amount Paid

ANSWER SHEET

When you buy something, the price is how much it costs. The amount paid is the money you give to the cashier. If you pay more than the price, the cashier gives you back the extra money, called the change. To find the change, subtract the price from the amount you paid. It's like if you have $10, buy something for $7, and get $3 back as change!

Choose the correct answer for each question below. Need help? Try Google.

1. If you buy a book for $15 and pay with a $20 bill, how much change will you receive?
   a. $10
   b. $5
   c. $3

2. You purchased a shirt for $25 and gave the cashier $30. What is the amount of change you should get back?
   a. $10
   b. $5
   c. $2

3. A movie ticket costs $12. If you pay $20, how much change will you receive?
   a. $8
   b. $7
   c. $5

4. You ordered a pizza for $18 and paid with a $50 bill. What is your change?
   a. $28
   b. $25
   c. $32

5. If a sandwich costs $9 and you pay with a $10 bill, how much change do you get?
   a. $3
   b. $2
   c. $1

6. You buy a coffee for $4.50 and give the cashier $5. What is your change?
   a. $0.50
   b. $0.25
   c. $1

7. A video game costs $60. If you pay $100, how much change will you receive?
   a. $30
   b. $50
   c. $40

8. You buy a dress for $45 and pay with a $100 bill. How much change do you get back?
   a. $60
   b. $55
   c. $50

9. If a bag of groceries costs $75 and you pay with a $100 bill, what is your change?
   a. $20
   b. $30
   c. $25

10. You pay $18 for a meal and give the waiter a $20 bill. How much is your change?
    a. $3
    b. $1
    c. $2

Test Your Knowledge Answer Key

Part 1: Parts of Speech

1. False. A verb is a word that describes an action or a state of being. A noun is a person, place, thing, or idea.
2. C. Blue - An adjective is a word that describes or modifies a noun.
3. Slept - This is the action the cat is performing.

Part 2: Verb Tenses

4. False. The past perfect tense describes an action that has happened before another action in the past.
5. Is running - The present progressive tense indicates an ongoing action happening right now.
6. Had - The correct form is "had already started," using the past perfect tense to show the movie starting happened before the arrival at the cinema.

Part 3: Sentence Structure

7. False. A compound sentence contains two or more independent clauses, and may be joined by a coordinating conjunction (for, and, nor, but, or, yet, so). A complex sentence contains one independent clause and one or more dependent clauses.
8. Flowers - Even though "flowers" comes after "bloom," it's what's doing the blooming, so it's the subject.
9. Answers may vary. Example: "Although I studied hard, I didn't do well on the test."

Part 4: Punctuation

10. True. A semicolon can be used to connect two closely related independent clauses that could stand alone as separate sentences if needed.
11. B. "Let's eat, grandma!" - The comma is necessary to clearly separate the clauses and avoid confusion.
12. Corrected sentence: "She said, 'I'm sorry for your loss.'" - When dialogue is reported, it should be enclosed in quotation marks, with a comma indicating the pause before the spoken words.

Earth Science Crossword

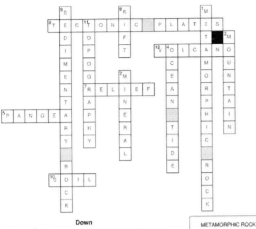

Across

5. supercontinent that scientists believe existed years ago
6. large sections of the Earth's crust that slowly move
7. elevation difference between different areas of a region
10. surface where plants grow
12. opening in the Earth's crust where molten rock erupts

Down

1. formed from great heat and pressure inside the Earth's crust
2. is a solid substance that occurs naturally
3. geological landform that rises significantly above the surrounding land
4. The rising and falling of sea levels
8. place where the Earth's crust is being pulled apart
9. Rocks formed from years of sediment
11. the physical features of an area of land

> METAMORPHIC ROCK
> MOUNTAIN SOIL
> PANGEA TECTONIC
> PLATES VOLCANO
> SEDIMENTARY ROCK
> MINERAL RELIEF RIFT
> TOPOGRAPHY OCEAN
> TIDE

The First Thanksgiving

The First Thanksgiving was a feast in 1621 where the Pilgrims and the Wampanoag Native Americans celebrated a successful harvest together. It marked a time of cooperation and sharing between the two groups. This event is considered the beginning of the Thanksgiving tradition in the United States.

Need help? Try Google or your favorite search engine.

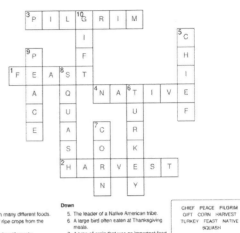

Across

1. A large meal with many different foods.
2. The gathering of ripe crops from the fields.
3. One of the English settlers who celebrated the First Thanksgiving
4. A person originally from a particular place, like the Wampanoag.

Down

5. The leader of a Native American tribe.
6. A large bird often eaten at Thanksgiving meals.
7. A type of grain that was an important food for both Pilgrims and Native Americans.
8. A vegetable that was part of the First Thanksgiving feast
9. A time without conflict or war, like when the Pilgrims and Wampanoag came together.
10. Something given to someone without expecting anything in return, symbolizing sharing and kindness.

> CHIEF PEACE PILGRIM
> GIFT CORN HARVEST
> TURKEY FEAST NATIVE
> SQUASH

Today Is Spelling Day!

Circle the correct spelling word then write it in cursive on the line provided.

	A	B	C	D
1.	bandadge	bandadje	**bandage**	bandaje
2.	**chest**	chesst	cheast	chast
3.	dripht	drnpht	drrift	**drift**
4.	dul	**dull**	voll	dol
5.	dussk	dusck	dossk	**dusk**
6.	stratch	strretch	**stretch**	straatch
7.	**flock**	flok	fllock	flok
8.	flnd	funo	**fond**	fpnd
9.	measure	maessure	maesure	**measure**
10.	cactos	cactos	cactus	**cactus**
11.	**scrap**	scrrap	scrrep	screp
12.	**shift**	shifft	shiphft	shipht
13.	smash	smesh	**smash**	smaash
14.	**switch**	swyltch	swytch	swittch
15.	sweptt	sweptt	**swept**	swapt
16.	threat	threat	**threat**	threat
17.	tymid	tymiwd	tmir	**timid**
18.	plliad	**plaid**	pllaid	pliad
19.	trust	**trust**	trost	trrost
20.	twist	twyst	twisst	**twist**

Coronavirus Outbreak Pandemic

If you've been around adults, you've probably heard a lot of talk about "coronavirus." This virus has evolved into a new __strain__ that is spreading throughout the world. It is called a coronavirus because the Latin word "corona" means "crown." Additionally, the virus appears to be wearing a spiky crown.

Generally, it causes coughing, fatigue, and a fever. However it can be extremely dangerous for the __elderly__ and those with other medical conditions. COVID-19 is the name of the virus that causes the disease.

In December 2019, Wuhan, a city in __China__ was the first place to discover the virus. However, we believe this virus originated in bats. It then hopped into another type of animal, passing it on to humans. Nobody knows for sure what this mysterious animal was, but some believe it was a pangolin, a scaly animal that feeds on ants.

The virus enters __cells__ via a unique "door" located on the exterior of human cells. Additionally, the new coronavirus requires a "key" to enter cells. The coronavirus, in this case, has a unique "spike" on its surface that it uses as a key to open the door.

Viruses cause illness by either killing human cells or impairing their function. As previously stated, the new coronavirus enters cells via a unique door. These unique entry points are located on cells in the __nose__ and lungs. If the virus multiplies too rapidly in the lungs, breathing can be difficult. This is referred to as pneumonia.

Fortunately, your body is equipped with an army to combat germs like coronavirus. It is referred to as the immune __system__. When a virus enters your body, it is attacked by your immune system. You know how when you're sick, you can develop a fever, a headache, or a runny nose? That is the result of the immune system, and it is beneficial! These unpleasant symptoms indicate that your body is battling the virus.

The majority of people who contract COVID-19 experience only mild __symptoms__ such as a cough, fever, or runny nose. Doctors are unsure why some people become extremely ill. Certain individuals' immune systems may not be strong enough. Other people's immune systems may be overly aggressive, causing damage to their own cells. Both of these factors have the potential to make people sicker.

There is a special test to determine whether or not you have COVID-19. Inform your parents if you become ill. They will contact your __physician__ to decide whether or not you require the test. It's similar to a flu test; they insert a Q-tip into your nose and examine your snot for the presence of the virus. The results are returned the following day.

Once inside cells, the virus multiplies rapidly. These virus copies replicate outside of cells and then infect other cells. When our normal cells are __bombarded__ with so many virus particles, they lose their ability to function properly... and we become ill.

By washing your hands, you can help prevent the spread of the virus. This involves __lathering__ up with soap and rubbing your hands together to thoroughly clean all of your fingers, under the fingernails, and between the fingers. You can sing the ABCs or create a new tune lasting approximately 20 seconds.

Additionally, remember to cough or sneeze into your elbow (as if you were a vampire!) and stay home if you are sick.

Put Decimal Numbers in Order

Putting decimal numbers in order means arranging them from smallest to largest, or the other way around. First, look at the numbers to the left of the decimal point; the smaller that number, the smaller the whole decimal. If those numbers are the same, then look at the digits right after the decimal point. Compare each digit in order until you find a difference—the smallest digit means the smallest decimal. Line up the decimals in order based on what you find, and you'll have them neatly arranged!

Choose the correct answer for each question below. Need more help? Try Google.

1. Which of the following decimal numbers is the largest?
   a. 4.7
   b. 4.6
   c. 4.5

2. Put the following numbers in order from smallest to largest: 2.3, 2.1, 2.5
   a. 2.5, 2.3, 2.1
   b. 2.3, 2.5, 2.1
   c. 2.1, 2.3, 2.5

3. Which of these numbers is the smallest?
   a. 3.04
   b. 3.14
   c. 3.4

4. Arrange the following in ascending order: 1.25, 1.5, 1.1
   a. 1.1, 1.25, 1.5
   b. 1.25, 1.1, 1.5
   c. 1.5, 1.25, 1.1

5. Which decimal is greater than 0.75?
   a. 0.6
   b. 0.8
   c. 0.7

6. Order these decimals from largest to smallest: 0.5, 0.05, 0.55
   a. 0.5, 0.55, 0.05
   b. 0.55, 0.5, 0.05
   c. 0.05, 0.5, 0.55

7. Which number is smaller than 0.3?
   a. 0.4
   b. 0.25
   c. 0.35

8. Put these numbers in order from largest to smallest: 5.1, 5.01, 5.001
   a. 5.01, 5.1, 5.001
   b. 5.001, 5.01, 5.1
   c. 5.1, 5.01, 5.001

9. Which decimal is equal to 1.5?
   a. 1.50
   b. 1.5
   c. 1.55

10. Arrange these decimals in ascending order: 0.9, 0.99, 0.8
    a. 0.99, 0.9, 0.8
    b. 0.9, 0.8, 0.99
    c. 0.8, 0.9, 0.99

Alphabetize and Define

Word bank
meter
irony
personification
denotation
onomatopoeia
alliteration
rhyme
metaphor
theme
symbolism
repetition
simile
stanza
connotation
imagery

1. alliteration
2. connotation
3. denotation
4. imagery
5. irony
6. metaphor
7. meter
8. onomatopoeia
9. personification
10. repetition
11. rhyme
12. simile
13. stanza
14. symbolism
15. theme

After putting the words in alphabetical order, choose 5 and write a definition in the space provided.

[Student worksheet has a 5 line writing exercise here.]

Predicting Weather

Sentence Building: Unscramble the sentences!

(Use a separate sheet of paper to write out sentences if needed.)

1. Predicting weather, also known as meteorology, involves the use of scientific principles and advanced technologies to forecast atmospheric conditions.

   technologies · advanced · of · the · meteorology, · and · involves · weather, · atmospheric · as · Predicting · conditions, · also · forecast · known · scientific · use · principles

2. Meteorologists analyze data from various sources, including satellite imagery, radar systems, and weather stations, to understand current weather patterns.

   sources, · stations, · current · radar · to · systems, · understand · including · imagery, · patterns. · various · analyze · data · from · and · Meteorologists · weather · weather · satellite

3. They utilize computer models that simulate the atmosphere's behavior, allowing them to make predictions about future weather events.

   behavior, · future · make · They · to · computer · them · about · simulate · the · weather · utilize · predictions · atmosphere's · allowing · models · events. · that

4. These predictions can range from short-term forecasts, such as daily temperatures and precipitation, to long-term outlooks like seasonal climate trends.

   These · climate · precipitation, · long-term · like · seasonal · outlooks · forecasts, · short-term · to · range · trends. · can · as · from · such · and · temperatures · daily · predictions

5. Factors such as pressure systems, humidity, wind patterns, and geographic features all play crucial roles in shaping weather forecasts.

   pressure · play · as · wind · Factors · features · and · all · crucial · shaping · patterns, · systems, · in · roles · geographic · forecasts. · weather · such · humidity,

6. As technology advances, the accuracy of weather predictions continues to improve, helping communities prepare for severe weather and making informed decisions.

   informed · to · severe · and · technology · advances, · continues · the · As · decisions. · communities · of · weather · helping · predictions · prepare · improve, · for · making · weather · accuracy

---

The Transcontinental Railroad

During this exercise, fill in the blanks with the correct word. Need help? Try Google or your favorite search engine.

coasts	constructed	Tunnel	continent	Steam
Union	vehicle	Bridge	Golden	Railroad
Journey	Central	Tracks	rails	Transport

1. Railroad - A track with rails on which trains run.
2. Transcontinental - Stretching across a continent.
3. Train - A vehicle that runs on tracks and carries people or goods.
4. Tracks - The rails on which a train travels.
5. Golden Spike - The final spike driven into the railroad to complete it.
6. Builders - People who constructed the railroad.
7. Bridge - A structure built to allow the train to cross over rivers or valleys.
8. Tunnel - A passage built through mountains for the train to pass.
9. Laying Tracks - The process of placing the rails on the ground.
10. Steam - What powered the early trains.
11. Union Pacific - One of the companies that built the railroad from the east.
12. Central Pacific - The company that built the railroad from the west.
13. Connection - Bringing the two coasts together with the railroad.
14. Transport - Moving people or goods from one place to another.
15. Journey - Traveling from one place to another, often made easier by the railroad.

Math Terms Matching

ANSWER SHEET

Match each math term to the correct meaning.

1	A	Rectangle	→	A parallelogram with four right angles.
2	G	Negative Number	→	A number less than zero.
3	C	Triangle	→	A three-sided polygon.
4	D	X	→	The Roman numeral for 10.
5	P	X-Axis	→	The horizontal axis in a coordinate plane.
6	B	Weight	→	The measure of how heavy something is.
7	M	Like Fractions	→	Fractions with the same denominator.
8	K	Like Terms	→	____ with the same variable and same exponents/powers.
9	F	Mode	→	The ____ is a list of numbers are the values that occur most frequently.
10	H	Midpoint	→	A point that is exactly halfway between two locations.
11	E	Line	→	A straight infinite path joining an infinite number of points in both directions.
12	I	Numerator	→	The top number in a fraction.
13	O	Octagon	→	A polygon with eight sides.
14	N	Logic	→	Sound reasoning and the formal laws of reasoning.
15	Q	Outcome	→	Used in probability to refer to the result of an event.
16	J	Polynomial	→	The sum of two or more monomials.
17	L	Quotient	→	The solution to a division problem.
18	R	Proper Fraction	→	A fraction whose denominator is greater than its numerator.

SUPERLATIVE ADJECTIVES

ANSWER SHEET

A superlative adjective is a comparative adjective that describes something as being of the highest degree or extreme. When comparing three or more people or things, we use superlative adjectives. Superlative adjectives typically end in 'est'. Examples of superlative adjectives include the words biggest and fastest.

Unscramble Word Tip: Try solving the easy words first, and then go back and answer the more difficult ones.

prettiest	hottest	crowded	friendliest	biggest	smallest
saddest	best	worst	tallest	shortest	longest
fattest	newest	heaviest	nicest	beautiful	expensive
cheapest	comfortable	youngest	largest		

1. peehtsac — c h e a p e s t
2. talresg — l a r g e s t
3. ntogels — l o n g e s t
4. wsenet — n e w e s t
5. icetns — n i c e s t
6. tstosreh — s h o r t e s t
7. samisetl — s m a l l e s t
8. lstteal — t a l l e s t
9. goysunte — y o u n g e s t
10. tggsbie — b i g g e s t
11. eftastt — f a t t e s t

12. ttoesht — h o t t e s t
13. adstdes — s a d d e s t
14. filtaubeu — b e a u t i f u l
15. ctlefarbmoo — c o m f o r t a b l e
16. ddrwoce — c r o w d e d
17. enpsvxeei — e x p e n s i v e
18. esdeirfiltn — f r i e n d l i e s t
19. hitvseea — h e a v i e s t
20. espttriel — p r e t t i e s t
21. bets — b e s t
22. wrsot — w o r s t

Introduction to Atoms

ANSWER SHEET

During this exercise, fill in the blanks with the correct word. Need help? Try Google or your favorite search engine.

Electrons	chemical	three	destroyed	nucleus
negative	small	Neutrons	empty	molecules
Protons	tiny	properties	matter	microscopes

1. Atoms are the _tiny_ building blocks that make up everything around us, from the air we breathe to the food we eat.
2. An atom is the smallest unit of matter that retains the _properties_ of an element, like gold or oxygen.
3. Atoms are tiny particles that are so small you can't see them with your eyes, only through special _microscopes_ .
4. Atoms are the basic units that make up all the _chemical_ elements on the periodic table, like hydrogen and helium.
5. An atom is made up of _three_ main parts.
6. The center of an atom, called the _nucleus_ , contains protons and neutrons.
7. _Electrons_ are tiny particles that orbit around the nucleus, much like planets orbiting the sun.
8. _Protons_ , found in the nucleus, have a positive electrical charge
9. Electrons, which move around the nucleus, have a _negative_ electrical charge
10. _Neutrons_ , also in the nucleus, have no electrical charge, they are neutral.
11. Everything you can touch, see, _smell_ , or taste is made of atoms joined together.
12. Atoms can join together to form _molecules_ , which are groups of atoms bonded together.
13. Atoms can change forms but cannot be created or _destroyed_ in ordinary chemical reactions.
14. Most of an atom is _empty_ space, with a tiny dense nucleus in the center and electrons zooming around it.
15. Even though we can't see atoms, they are incredibly powerful and essential for the structure and function of all _matter_ .

The New Deal

ANSWER SHEET

First, read all the way through. After that, go back and fill in the blanks. You can skip the blanks you're unsure about and finish them later.

harvests	public	economic	farmers	country's
crisis	President	Social	government	Civilian

The New Deal was a series of programs and policies introduced by _President_ Franklin D. Roosevelt to help the United States recover from the Great Depression. The Great Depression was a severe economic _crisis_ that began in 1929 and caused widespread unemployment, poverty, and suffering.

When Franklin D. Roosevelt became President in 1933, he promised to take action and help the country get back on its feet. The New Deal included many different programs aimed at providing jobs, supporting _farmers_ , and helping people in need.

One of the key parts of the New Deal was the creation of _public_ works projects. These were large construction projects that provided jobs for millions of Americans. People built roads, bridges, schools, and parks. These projects not only gave people work but also improved the _country's_ infrastructure.

Another important part of the New Deal was the _Social_ Security Act. This program provided financial support to elderly people, the disabled, and unemployed workers. It helped ensure that people had some money to live on even if they couldn't work.

The New Deal also included programs to help farmers. Many farmers were struggling because of low crop prices and poor _harvests_ . The government offered loans and subsidies to help them keep their farms running and support their families.

Additionally, the New Deal established agencies like the _Civilian_ Conservation Corps (CCC) and the Works Progress Administration (WPA). The CCC put young men to work in national parks and forests, planting trees and building trails. The WPA hired artists, writers, and musicians to create public art and perform in communities.

The New Deal didn't solve all the problems of the Great Depression, but it provided hope and relief to many Americans. It showed that the _government_ could take action to help people in times of need. President Roosevelt's New Deal left a lasting impact on the country and laid the foundation for future social and _economic_ programs.

Numbers Vocabulary: Math, Time, & Money Study Guide

1	C	Add	→	to put something with something else or with a group of other things; to increase the amount or cost of something: if you add numbers or amounts together, you calculate their total≠ subtract
2	E	ATM	→	abbreviation for automated teller machine: a machine outside a bank that you use to get money from your account
3	N	Borrow	→	to use something, often money, that belongs to someone else and that you must give back to them later; to take or copy someone's ideas, words etc. and use them in your own work, language etc.≠lend, loan
4	W	Cardinal Number	→	a number such as 1, 2, or 3, that shows how many of something there are, but not what order they are in ≠ Ordinal Number
5	U	Cash	→	money in the form of coins or notes rather than checks, credit cards etc.; money (noun); to exchange a check etc. for cash (verb)
6	B	Change	→	the money that you get back when you have paid for something with more money than it costs; money in the form of coins, not paper money (noun); to become different, or to make something become different; to take off your clothes and put on different ones (verb)
7	P	Check	→	a printed piece of paper that you write an amount of money on, sign, and use instead of money to pay for things (noun); to do something in order to find out whether something really is correct, true, or in good condition; to make a mark (✓) next to an answer, something on a list etc. to show you have chosen it, that it is correct, or that you have dealt with it (verb)
8	H	Clockwise	→	in the same direction as the hands of a clock move ≠ counterclockwise
9	V	Counterclockwise	→	in the opposite direction to the way in which the hands of a clock move around; anticlockwise ≠ counterclockwise
10	D	Daylight Saving Time	→	the time during the summer when clocks are one hour ahead of standard time; daylight savings
11	F	Debit Card	→	a plastic card with your signature on it, that resembles a credit card, but functions like a check and through which payments for purchases or services are made electronically to pay for things, the money is taken directly from your bank account
12	T	Deposit	→	a part of the cost of something you are buying that you pay some time before you pay the rest of it; money that you pay when you rent something such as an apartment or car, which will be given back if you do not damage it; an amount of money that is paid into a bank account ≠ withdrawal (noun); to put money or something valuable in a bank or other place where it will be safe; to put something down in a particular place (verb)
13	S	Divide	→	if something divides, or if you divide it, it separates into two or more parts; to keep two areas separate from each other; to calculate how many times one number contains a smaller number; to make people disagree so that they form groups with different opinions
14	K	Equal	→	the same in size, number, amount, value etc. as something else; equivalent; having the same rights, opportunities etc. as everyone else, whatever your race, religion, or sex
15	I	Equivalent	→	having the same value, purpose, job etc. as a person or thing of a different kind (adj.); something that has the same value, purpose, job etc. as something else; something that is equal in value, amount, quality etc. to something else (noun)
16	O	Fraction	→	a very small amount of something; a part of a whole number in mathematics, such as ½ or ⅝
17	G	Lend	→	to let someone borrow money or something that belongs to you for a short time; if a bank or financial institution lends money, it lets someone have it on condition that they pay it back later, often gradually, with an additional amount as interest ≠borrow
18	M	Measure	→	to find the size, length, or amount of something, using standard units such as inches, meters etc.; to judge the importance, value, or true nature of something; if a piece of equipment measures something, it shows or records a particular kind of measurement
19	O	Measurement	→	the length, height etc. of something; the act of measuring something
20	X	Ordinal Number	→	one of the numbers such as first, second, third etc. which show the order of things ≠ Cardinal Number
21	J	Receipt	→	a piece of paper that you are given which shows that you have paid for something; when someone receives something
22	A	Roman Numeral	→	a number in a system first used in ancient Rome that uses combinations of the letters I, V, X, L, C, D, and M to represent numbers ≠ Arabic numeral
23	L	Subtract	→	to take a number or an amount from a larger number or amount; deduct; minus
24	R	Time Zone	→	one of the 24 areas that the world is divided into, each of which has its own time
25	Y	Withdraw	→	to take money out of a bank account; to stop taking part in an activity, belonging to an organization etc.; or to make someone do this

It's Sentence Building Day!

Practice *sentence* building. *Unscramble* the words to form a complete sentence.

1. When a volcano erupts it kills the plant life around it.

   it · around · plant · it · When · kills · volcano · life · erupts · the · it

2. I eat one banana every day.

   I · banana · one · eat · every · day.

3. The term locomotion means movement or travel.

   or · travel. · locomotion · term · movement · means · The

4. Our teacher says repetition will help us learn.

   says · learn. · teacher · repetition · help · us · will · Our

5. What is all the commotion about?

   about? · What · commotion · is · all · the

6. I have to maintain good grades or my car will be taken away.

   have · away. · car · taken · good · maintain · my · will · grades · I · be · to · or

7. The monkey was curious about the person's camera.

   person's · about · monkey · The · curious · camera. · was · the

8. I know I am becoming dehydrated so I should drink water.

   becoming · should · am · drink · so · dehydrated · I · know · water. · I · I

9. I will confiscate all of your candy now.

   your · will · I · now. · all · confiscate · candy · of

10. Our countries' governments are trying to do what's best for the people.

    to · countries' · trying · Our · best · are · do · the · what's · governments · for · people.

11. Amethyst is a semiprecious stone.

    semiprecious · is · Amethyst · a · stone.

Fascinating Stars

First, read all the way through. After that, go back and fill in the blanks. You can skip the blanks you're unsure about and finish them later.

| temperature | patterns | temperatures | balls | Earth |
| outer | explode | hydrogen | atmosphere | nebulae |

Stars are fascinating, twinkling objects in the night sky. They are giant balls of glowing gas, mostly hydrogen and helium, and they produce light and heat through a process called nuclear fusion.

How Stars are Born
Stars are born in huge clouds of gas and dust called nebulae . When parts of these clouds collapse under their own gravity, they heat up and start to glow, forming a new star. This process can take millions of years!

Types of Stars
Stars come in different sizes, colors, and temperatures . Here are a few types:

1. Red Dwarfs: These are small and cool stars. They are the most common type of star in the universe and can live for trillions of years.
2. Yellow Dwarfs: Our Sun is a yellow dwarf. These stars are medium-sized and have a moderate temperature. They can live for about 10 billion years.
3. Blue Giants: These are large and very hot stars. They are blue because they burn at very high temperatures. Blue giants have shorter lifespans, often only a few million years.
4. Supergiants: Even bigger than blue giants, supergiants are some of the largest stars in the universe. They can explode in massive supernovae at the end of their lives.

The Life Cycle of a Star
Stars go through a life cycle:

1. Formation: Stars begin their life in a nebula.
2. Main Sequence: This is the longest stage of a star's life where it burns hydrogen into helium. Our Sun is currently in this stage.
3. Red Giant or Supergiant: When stars exhaust their hydrogen, they expand and cool down to become red giants or supergiants.
4. End of Life: Stars end their lives differently depending on their size. Smaller stars may shed their outer layers and leave behind a white dwarf. Larger stars might explode in a supernova, leaving behind a neutron star or a black hole.

Constellations
Stars often appear to form patterns in the sky, called constellations. Ancient people named these patterns after animals, mythological characters, and objects. For example, Orion is a famous constellation that looks like a hunter.

Fun Facts
· Distances: Stars are very far away from us. The closest star to Earth , other than the Sun, is Proxima Centauri, which is about 4.24 light-years away.
· Twinkling: Stars appear to twinkle because of the Earth's atmosphere . As the light from stars passes through different layers of air, it bends and makes the stars seem to flicker.
· Star Colors: A star's color tells us its temperature . Blue stars are hot, while red stars are cooler.

Stars are incredible, and studying them helps us learn more about the universe and our place in it. Next time you look at the night sky, think about the amazing journeys of these distant suns!

Nullification Crisis

1. The Nullification Crisis was a political _conflict_ in the United States that occurred between 1832 and 1833.

2. It was centered around the issue of states' rights versus _federal_ rights, particularly regarding the power to nullify or cancel federal laws.

3. The _crisis_ began when South Carolina declared that two federal tariffs (taxes on imported goods), passed in 1828 and 1832, were unconstitutional and, therefore, did not have to be obeyed within their state's borders.

4. These tariffs, known as the "Tariffs of Abominations," were seen as _benefitting_ the industrial North at the expense of the agricultural South.

5. South Carolina, led by Senator John C. Calhoun, _argued_ that states should have the right to nullify federal laws if they believed those laws were unconstitutional.

6. The Nullification Crisis was one of the earliest major _threats_ to the unity of the United States and foreshadowed the later Civil War.

7. In response to South Carolina's nullification act, _President_ Andrew Jackson declared it to be treasonous.

8. Jackson, a firm believer in the federal government's supremacy over the states, signed the Force Bill into law in 1833, giving him the power to use military force to _enforce_ federal laws in South Carolina.

9. The crisis was eventually resolved when _Congress_ passed a compromise bill known as the Compromise Tariff of 1833, which gradually lowered the tariffs.

10. John C. Calhoun was _Vice_ President under Andrew Jackson but resigned due to their differing views during the crisis.

11. The Nullification Crisis highlighted the growing tensions between the North and South over issues of states' rights and _slavery_.

12. The crisis was a key moment in the _development_ of the concept of secession or the idea that a state could choose to leave the Union.

13. The term "nullification" comes from the _Latin_ word "nullus," which means "none." It refers to the idea of making something legally null and void.

14. The crisis showed the potential dangers of a single state _defying_ federal law, setting the stage for future conflicts.

15. Despite the resolution of the crisis, the issues of states' rights and federal authority continued to be contentious topics in American politics, eventually contributing to the _outbreak_ of the Civil War.

Look It Up! Pop Quiz

Learn some basic vocabulary words that you will come across again and again in the course of your studies in algebra. By knowing the definitions of most algebra words, you will be able to construct and solve algebra problems much more easily.

Find the answer to the questions below by _looking up_ each word. (The wording can be tricky. Take your time.)

1. improper fraction
   a. a fraction that the denominator is equal to the numerator
   b. **a fraction in which the numerator is greater than the denominator, is always 1 or greater**

2. equivalent fraction
   a. a fraction that has a DIFFERENT value as a given fraction
   b. **a fraction that has the SAME value as a given fraction**

3. simplest form of fraction
   a. **an equivalent fraction for which the only common factor of the numerator and denominator is 1**
   b. an equivalent fraction for which the only least factor of the denominator is -1

4. mixed number
   a. **the sum of a whole number and a proper fraction**
   b. the sum of a variable and a fraction

5. reciprocal
   a. a number that can be divided by another number to make 10
   b. **a number that can be multiplied by another number to make 1**

6. percent
   a. a percentage that compares a number to 0.1
   b. **a ratio that compares a number to 100**

7. sequence
   a. a list of addition numbers that follow a operation
   b. **a set of numbers that follow a pattern**

8. arithmetic sequence
   a. **a sequence where EACH term is found by adding or subtracting the exact same number to the previous term**
   b. a sequence where NO term is found by multiplying the exact same number to the previous term

9. geometric sequence
   a. **a sequence where each term is found by multiplying or dividing by the exact same number to the previous term**
   b. a sequence where each term is found by adding or dividing by a different number to the previous term

10. order of operations
    a. **the procedures to follow when simplifying a numerical expression**
    b. the procedure to follow when adding any fraction by 100

11. variable expression
    a. **a mathematical phrase that contains variables, numbers, and operation symbols**
    b. a mathematical phrase that contains numbers and operation symbols

12. absolute value
    a. **the distance a number is from zero on the number line**
    b. the range a number is from one on the number line

13. integers
    a. **a set of numbers that includes whole numbers and their opposites**
    b. a set of numbers that includes whole numbers and their differences

14. x-axis
    a. **the horizontal number line that, together with the y-axis, establishes the coordinate plane**
    b. the vertical number line that, together with the y-axis, establishes the coordinate plane

15. y-axis
    a. **the vertical number line that, together with the x-axis, establishes the coordinate plane**
    b. the horizontal number line that, together with the x-axis, establishes the coordinate plane

16. coordinate plane
    a. plane formed by one number line that horizontally axis and the vertical x-axis intersecting at their 1 points
    b. **plane formed by two number lines (the horizontal x-axis and the vertical y-axis) intersecting at their zero points**

17. quadrant
    a. one of two sections on the four plane formed by the intersection of the x-axis
    b. **one of four sections on the coordinate plane formed by the intersection of the x-axis and the y-axis**

18. ordered pair
    a. **a pair of numbers that gives the location of a point in the coordinate plane. Also known as the "coordinates" of a point.**
    b. a pair of equal numbers that gives the range of a point in the axis plane. Also known as the y-axis of a point.

19. x-coordinate
    a. **the number that indicates the position of a point to the left or right of the y-axis**
    b. the number that indicates the range of a point to the left ONLY of the y-axis

20. y-coordinate
    a. **the number that indicates the position of a point above or below the x-axis**
    b. the number that indicates the value of a point above the x-axis

21. inverse operations
    a. operations that equal to each other
    b. **operations that undo each other**

22. inequality
    a. a math sentence that uses a letter (x or y) to indicate that the left and right sides of the sentence hold values that are different
    b. **a math sentence that uses a symbol (<, >, ≤, ≥, ≠) to indicate that the left and right sides of the sentence hold values that are different**

23. perimeter
    a. **the distance around the outside of a figure**
    b. the distance around the inside of a figure

24. circumference
    a. **the distance around a circle**
    b. the range around a circle

25. area
    a. **the number of square units inside a 2-dimensional figure**
    b. the number of square units inside a 3-dimensional figure

26. volume
    a. **the number of cubic units inside a 3-dimensional figure**
    b. the number of cubic squared units inside a 2-dimensional figure

27. radius
    a. a line segment that runs from the middle of the circle to end of the circle
    b. **a line segment that runs from the center of the circle to somewhere on the circle**

28. chord
    a. **a line segment that runs from somewhere on the circle to another place on the circle**
    b. a circle distance that runs from somewhere on the run left to another place on the circle

29. diameter
    a. **a chord that passes through the center of the circle**
    b. a line that passes through the end of the circle

30. mean
    a. the sum of the data items added by the number of data items minus 2
    b. **the sum of the data items divided by the number of data items**

31. median
    a. the first data item found after sorting the data items in descending order
    b. **the middle data item found after sorting the data items in ascending order**

32. mode
    a. **the data item that occurs most often**
    b. the data item that occurs less than two times

33. range
    a. **the difference between the highest and the lowest data item**
    b. the difference between the middle number and the lowest number item

34. outlier
    a. **a data item that is much higher or much lower than all the other data items**
    b. a data item that is much lower or less than all the other data items

35. ratio
    a. a comparison of two quantities by multiplication
    b. **a comparison of two quantities by division**

36. rate
    a. a ratio that has equal and the values not in the same units
    b. **a ratio that compares quantities measured in different units**

37. proportion
    a. a statement (ratio) showing two or more ratios to be equal
    b. **a statement (equation) showing two ratios to be equal**

38. outcomes
    a. **possible results of action**
    b. possible answer when two elements are the same

39. probability
    a. a ratio that explains the likelihood of the distance and miles between to places
    b. **a ratio that explains the likelihood of an event**

40. theoretical probability
    a. the probability of the highest favorable number of outcomes to possible outcomes (based on what is not expected to occur)
    b. **the ratio of the number of favorable outcomes to the number of possible outcomes (based on what is expected to occur)**

41. experimental probability
    a. the ratio of the number of times that 2 when an event occurs to the number of times times 2 an experiment is done (based on real experimental data)
    b. **the ratio of the number of times an event occurs to the number of times an experiment is done (based on real experimental data)**

42. distributive property
    a. a way to simplify an expression that contains a five term being added by a group of terms
    b. **a way to simplify an expression that contains a single term being multiplied by a group of terms**

43. term
    a. a number, a variable, or quotient of an equal number and a variable(s)
    b. **a number, a variable, or product of a number and a variable(s)**

44. constant
    a. **a term with no variable part (i.e. a number)**
    b. a term with no variable + y part (i.e. 4 + y)

45. coefficient
    a. a number that divides a variable
    b. **a number that multiplies a variable**

Are vs. Our

Depending on your exact pronunciation, it can sometimes be difficult for someone to tell whether you're saying "are" or "our."

Are is used in the English simple present tense. It shows that something exists. Are is also a helping verb. Are is pronounced like "arrr".

Our is the possessive form of we. The proper pronunciation of the word is two syllables, "oww-er".

Circle the correct answer.

1. **Our** [Are / Our] school holiday is two weeks long.

2. You **are** [are / our] very good at spelling.

3. **Are** [Our / Are] we going to the picnic?

4. As a school, we do **our** [are / our] best to meet the needs of every student.

5. We **are** [our / are] driving to visit a friend.

6. We went to the dog shelter and picked out **our** [are / our] new dog together.

7. We **are** [are / our] going to win the band contest this year.

8. After the terrible breakup, he realized that there **are** [our / are] other fish in the sea.

9. When the homeowners opened the door, they exclaimed, "Welcome to **our** [are / our] house!"

10. Since everyone shared it, the family called it **"our** ["our / are] car."

11. The Smiths **are** [our / are] very wealthy people.

12. There **are** [our / are] sixty minutes in an hour.

13. **Our** [Our / We] school holiday is two weeks long.

Battle of Yorktown

Long, long ago, in a land that's now our very own backyard, a battle took place that would change the course of history forever. This battle was known as the Battle of Yorktown, and it marked the **end** of a fierce and fiery period known as the American Revolution.

Imagine a giant game of chess, but instead of playing on a small board, the players used the entire city of Yorktown as their **battlefield**. The British, led by General Lord Cornwallis, were the red pieces, and the Americans, along with their French allies, were the blue pieces. The generals moved their soldiers like chess pieces, each one trying to outsmart the other.

The American general, George Washington, was like a clever fox. He had a secret weapon - his French friend, **General** Rochambeau. Together, they hatched a plan as sly as a fox sneaking into a chicken coop. They decided to surround Yorktown, cutting off any chance for the British soldiers to **escape** or get more supplies. It was like trapping a group of ants inside a circle drawn with chalk.

The **siege** of Yorktown lasted for several weeks. Can you imagine being stuck in your school for weeks with no new food supplies coming in? That's how it was for the British soldiers. Slowly but surely, like a cookie jar being emptied bit by bit, their strength and **morale** began to crumble.

Finally, on October 19, 1781, General Cornwallis knew he had no other choice but to **surrender**. He was supposed to hand over his sword to General Washington, but he was too embarrassed to face him. Instead, he sent his deputy, claiming he was ill. It was like a bully who talks big but runs away when it's time to face the **consequences**.

The Battle of Yorktown was a turning point in the American Revolution. It was the last major battle, and it effectively sealed America's victory. The brave and clever strategies of the American and **French** forces had paid off, just like when you work hard and smart to win a difficult game.

So, the next time you're playing a strategy game or planning a surprise for your friend, remember the Battle of Yorktown. It's a reminder that with courage, **clever** thinking, and the help of good friends, you can overcome even the biggest challenges and make history!

Atoms in Space

First, read all the way through. After that, go back and fill in the blanks. You can skip the blanks you're unsure about and finish them later.

atoms	gas	neutrons	iron	Stars
nuclear	vacuum	nucleus	nebulae	universe

Imagine looking up at the night sky and seeing all those twinkling stars. Did you know that everything you see up there, from stars to planets, is made of tiny particles called **atoms**? Atoms are the building blocks of everything in the universe, including space itself!

Atoms are incredibly small. In fact, they are so tiny that millions of them can fit on the tip of a pin! Each atom is made up of a **nucleus**, which has protons and **neutrons**, and electrons that zoom around the nucleus like planets orbiting the sun.

In space, atoms combine to form all sorts of amazing things. **Stars**, for example, are giant balls of gas made primarily of hydrogen and helium atoms. These atoms collide and fuse together in a process called **nuclear** fusion, which releases a tremendous amount of energy and makes the stars shine brightly.

Planets, moons, and asteroids are also made of atoms. The Earth, for instance, is composed of various elements like oxygen, silicon, and **iron**, each made of their own unique atoms. These atoms bond together to form rocks, water, air, and everything else that makes up our planet.

Even the vast emptiness of space, known as the **vacuum**, isn't completely empty. It contains sparse atoms and subatomic particles floating around. Sometimes, clouds of **gas** and dust in space, called **nebulae**, are made of these atoms. These nebulae can eventually come together to form new stars and planets.

Scientists study atoms in space to learn more about the **universe**. By understanding how atoms interact and form different structures, we can discover the secrets of stars, galaxies, and even the origins of life itself.

So, whenever you gaze at the stars, remember that those distant lights are made of the same tiny atoms that make up everything here on Earth. The universe is a vast, atom-filled playground waiting to be explored!

ADDITIONAL ASSIGNMENTS PLANNER

○ MONDAY

GOALS THIS WEEK

○ TUESDAY

○ WEDNESDAY

WHAT TO STUDY

○ THURSDAY

○ FRIDAY

EXTRA CREDIT WEEKEND WORK
○ SATURDAY / SUNDAY

ADDITIONAL ASSIGNMENTS PLANNER

○ MONDAY

GOALS THIS WEEK

○ TUESDAY

○ WEDNESDAY

WHAT TO STUDY

○ THURSDAY

○ FRIDAY

EXTRA CREDIT WEEKEND WORK
○ SATURDAY / SUNDAY

ADDITIONAL ASSIGNMENTS PLANNER

○ MONDAY

GOALS THIS WEEK

○ TUESDAY

○ WEDNESDAY

WHAT TO STUDY

○ THURSDAY

○ FRIDAY

EXTRA CREDIT WEEKEND WORK
○ SATURDAY / SUNDAY

ADDITIONAL ASSIGNMENTS PLANNER

○ MONDAY

GOALS THIS WEEK

○ TUESDAY

○ WEDNESDAY

WHAT TO STUDY

○ THURSDAY

○ FRIDAY

EXTRA CREDIT WEEKEND WORK
○ SATURDAY / SUNDAY

Coloring Page: Medieval Architecture in Western Europe

MAZE

Coloring Page: Swan

Pirate

Connect the dots

Coloring Page: Viking Woman

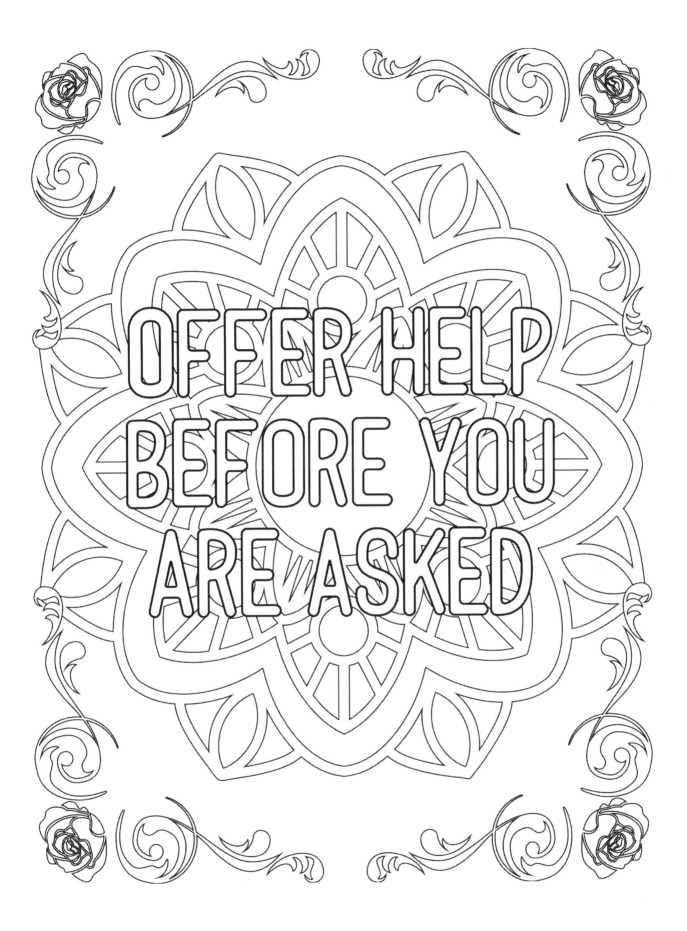

REPORT CARD

THIS WILL BE AN AMAZING SCHOOL YEAR!

Name: _____

Year: _____

Teacher: _____

Grading Period: _____

SUBJECT	GRADE	FEEDBACK
Arts		
Computer		
English		
History		
Math		
Music		
Science		
Social Studies		
Physical Education		

GRADING SCALE:

A+ = 96-100
A = 91-95
B+ = 86-90
B = 81-85

C = 76-80
D = 75 - 70
FAIL = 69 and below

TOTAL DAYS OF SCHOOL:

Days Attended:

Days Absent:

End of the Year Evaluation

Name: _____

Grade/Level: _____ Date: _____

Subjects Studied: _____

_____

_____

Cut out book

Goals Accomplished: _____

_____

_____

_____

Most Improved Areas:_____

_____

_____

_____

Areas of Improvement:_____

_____

_____

Main Curriculum Evaluation	Satisfied		A= Above Standards S= Meets Standards N= Needs Improvement	Final Grades
_____	Yes	No	98-100 A+ 93-97 A	_____
_____	Yes	No	90-92 A 88-89 B+	_____
_____	Yes	No	83-87 B 80-82 B	_____
_____	Yes	No	78-79 C+ 73-77 C 70-72 C	_____
_____	Yes	No	68-69 D+ 62-67 D	_____
_____	Yes	No	60-62 D 59 & Below F	_____

Most Enjoyed:_____

_____

Least Enjoyed:_____

_____

GRADES TRACKER

Week	Monday	Tuesday	Wednesday	Thursday	Friday
1					
2					
3					
4					
5					
6					
7					
8					
9					
10					
11					
12					
13					
14					
15					
16					
17					
18					

Notes

Made in the USA
Columbia, SC
13 December 2024

49201220R00057